Contents

27

14

5

16

20
37

12   9
38

18

2

Preface

What Rights Should Minorities Have?

Conor Cruise O'Brien

What rights should minorities have, apart from the rights they actually claim? Or can separation be maintained in practice at all rigidly? Certainly there is no use telling a minority it should have rights which in fact it does not want, or which it feels to be irrelevant to its actual needs and situation. And the rights which minorities have actually claimed vary very widely indeed.

Many minorities have asserted and maintained for periods of varying length a right to rule over majorities. The British in India, the Afrikaaners in South Africa, East European Communist parties and the West Nile soldiery in Uganda are all examples of this assertion of that kind of right.

This claim of right has been grounded in theory on genetic, theological and ideological conceptions, and in practice most often on superior fire-power. It may be said that the right of a particular minority to rule over a majority is no right at all but an arrogant pretension. In terms of liberal and democratic values this is certainly so. But some uncomfortable considerations enter here. For is not a commitment to liberal and democratic values in itself a characteristic of a minority, quite a small minority, as it would appear, of the inhabitants of this planet? That being so, by exactly what right do we tell or try to tell or think about telling other minorities what their rights are and what they are not. By what right? Not by any democratic right, certainly. We tell, let us say, the Tutsi that the right he fancies he possesses to dominate the Hutu is not a real right. He replies in effect that as far as his culture is concerned, it *is* a right. (I am taking Tutsi and Hutu virtually at random, and I hope no expert in that area of the world

Prefacexi

will take me up too literally! We should guard our flanks at all times!) We tell him it is not a right, because it is contrary to democracy, to which our ancestors became converted in the nineteenth century, along with imperialism (although we might leave that out so as not to confuse the Tutsi!) He says his ancestors did not become so converted, and are we claiming that our ancestors were superior to his? Now, that is a forked question, and we have to be very careful how we answer it. If we say, 'No, no, of course not, my dear fellow,' he can ask us: by what right then are we telling him that he must act according to the acquired convictions of our ancestors who are admittedly no better than his own? If, on the other hand, we say, yes, our people represent a more advanced stage of civilization than his do, he replies that this is exactly his own position in relation to the Hutu.

That is an imaginary discussion, but it does, I think, illustrate — in I hope what you will not feel is too flippant a way when we are discussing a very serious question — a real difficulty inherent in attempting to define, from within a particular historical phase of a particular culture, norms applicable universally in respect of minorities or anything else, in widely scattered and diverse human conditions and situations about which, generally speaking, our knowledge has to be — and most certainly mine is — very limited. It would take the nerve of an early nineteenth-century missionary explorer to set about such a task with full conviction. We do not have that kind of nerve any more, but neither, fortunately, have we acquired the opposite kind of nerve, the nerve to say, with Nietzsche, 'There are whole peoples who have failed', and to be entirely indifferent to their lot. European ideas about the underdeveloped world have, I think, never been so uncertain and so tentative as they are now. The certainties of imperialism are gone — I think — but so are the certainties of anti-imperialism: the bright hopes of decolonisation, the notion of the transforming power of technical aid, the charisma of a great convergence of a world revolution. All these ideas are still around, but one senses a certain lack of conviction in relation to them. We are groping, not quite certain that we have even the right to grope, and more than half afraid of the things we may find among 'them', 'the other' and in ourselves. Yet we cannot help groping, sending and receiving faint and ambiguous signals. Sometimes, as in the case of Biafra, of Bangladesh, of the Uganda Asians, we or a number of us, are sufficiently moved by a particular signal to try to help in some way. And sometimes also, when we look back on that, we cannot be sure whether what we did actually hindered or helped.

The cases which have touched imaginations and consciences in Europe and America are mainly cases of minorities — not ruling minorities of course, but underdogs — people harassed in varying degrees and kinds ranging from the quiet but terrible social ostracism which surrounds the Burakumin in Japan to the waves of violent persecution experienced in turn by Bengali and Bihari in East Pakistan/Bangladesh, to take only fairly recent or contemporary examples. It is of these endangered or stigmatised minorities of course that we generally think when we ask what rights minorities should have.

Even in relation to such minorities only, and leaving aside the ruling kind, this question remains extraordinarily hard to answer. The rights which such minorities, or at least their spokesmen, have historically sought, include — and this is not an exhaustive list — first of all, social integration into the wider society, claimed at various times by certain American negro groups, Jews in nineteenth-century Germany and elsewhere and in the twentieth-century Soviet Union — at least at one time — Algerian Moslems in France at one time, Catholics in Northern Ireland at the time of the campaign for full British rights (1967–69) and West Indians in Britain at one time. We may take it too that this is what the people such as the Burakumin in Japan want, and that without this particular right other rights in their context can have little meaning for them. And this is a right which neither domestic law nor international convention can secure for them. In certain circumstances, however, some display of international interest may help. American blacks certainly benefited from this from the time of Little Rock on, and so also, although more ambiguously, did Northern Irish Catholics.

The second form of rights which minorities have sought and seek include economic, technical and functional integration including equality of access to training and promotion, but without much demand for fuller social integration. The Chinese of North America, the Pakistanis of Britain, are examples here. But in fact I think that most of those who have sought or seemed to seek social integration have also at different times been interested in this kind, and perhaps in some cases more in this kind than in the social integration that they seemed to be looking for. There can be notable ambiguities and deceptive appearances in this area. For example, when Northern Irish Catholic spokesmen demanded full British rights in 1968–69, they were not really, as they seemed to be, looking for assimilation into the British community; what they were really doing was more tactical: it was to turn the Ulster Protestant claim, 'Ulster is British', into a weapon against the internal realities of the Ulster Protestant state. Only four years later the right claimed by the same spokesmen was opposite in form: that of integration into a united Ireland. And it could reasonably be argued that the very different and contradictory rights indeed sought at different times were really instruments used to secure the only right that could have much practical meaning in the lives of those concerned, namely, economic and functional integration as defined here. In practice also the line between economic and social integration is hard to draw. To the extent that education is in common, it works, though imperfectly, towards social integration. If education is separate, the majority will not be easily convinced, or easily admit, that the schools of the minority can really give an adequate training to warrant the kind of access to jobs and promotion that the minority will accept as constituting equality of opportunity.

The third case is this: sometimes the right to which the minority comes to commit itself, often having tried other things with what it feels to be lack of success, is the diametrical opposite of integration, i.e. political secession. The same minority coping with different conditions may at one stage be committed to total integration and at another to complete secession. The Ibos of Nigeria are perhaps the most classical case of this in recent times.

Secession is of course the most doubtful and controversial of all minority rights, with the exception of the right claimed by certain minorities to rule over majorities. I am sure you will wish me to give particular attention to the question of whether, and if so, in what circumstances secession can constitute a right of a minority. This question affects the whole area of minority rights discussion. It is the dimension (if you like) which makes this so sensitive a subject.

Secession is a very unpopular idea, naturally so, since it threatens the life of a state and threatens public order. Yet hardly anyone I think would claim that there is no such thing as a right to secede in any circumstances at all. The nearest thing one gets to that position is, I think, in certain circles in the United States, where for more than a century the dominant tradition in the United States — that of the Northern victors in the Civil War — has of course been strongly anti-secessionist, yet could hardly deny the right of the American colonies to secede from the Empire of George III, or of what are now the Latin-American states to secede from Spain with the help of the United States. For a long time the distinction was made that it was all right to secede from the things called empires but all wrong to secede from things called republics. This distinction stood Woodrow Wilson in good stead when at the end of the First World War he threw in that great secessionist fragmentation bomb, the principle of the self-determination of nations (which was not, I may note in passing, applicable to the Irish at the time, though they made good use of the propaganda value of this declaration). In the wake of the First World War this was used to break up the defeated empires and after the Second World War it was applied to the territories of the British and French empires. But there was a difference. In the post-First World War division an attempt was made to build the new states as far as possible around historical, cultural and linguistic groupings, such as we have been accustomed to describe as nations. In the case of the post-Second World War division, hardly any corresponding effort to sort out peoples was attempted, and the arbitrary assumption was made, perhaps had to be made, that the various colonial administrative territories, all of short duration and some of vast extent, now constituted nations and were exercising self-determination. (You note that the meaning of the word 'self-determination' perceptibly changed at this point in time.) In fact some of the peoples included in these new nations, and some of those later anxious to escape from them, at least for a time, were more numerous than the population of some of the new states set up in Europe under self-determination at the end of the First World War.

It is hard to see, if we are putting the question on a moral plane (as I suppose we must if what we are attempting to discuss is rights), why self-determination should be right in the one case and necessarily wrong in the other. I believe that secession is an evil, or rather the recognition of an evil, a breakdown in human relations. I also believe that no minority is likely to have recourse to it, with all its dangers, unless the pressures on it are felt to be intolerable, and unless also other conditions apply in terms of numbers, terrain, diplomatic conjuncture and other apparently propitious factors. It would be uselessly pedantic, I believe, to draw up rules for when secession is a right. It is enough to say that no minority is likely to attempt anything like this unless it or a substantial section of it has been driven desperate by events. The Biafrans, for example, felt, after the Northern massacre of Ibos that they had — and they asserted this passionately — the same basic right to defend themselves as had, for example, the Jews of the Warsaw Ghetto. They may have been unwise in attempting secession, and it seems they were. They may have exaggerated the danger, and it now seems they did. But it would be hard to see on what grounds, granted the historical precedents in their particular situation, it could be said that they had no moral right to make their attempt.

The recognition of that right by others is, of course, another matter. That cynical old maxim about treason never prospering — 'Treason doth never prosper; what's the reason? That if it prosper none dares call it treason' — seems to apply here. Bangladesh is now recognised by all, Biafra by none. The reason is not that Bangladesh had necessarily a better moral case than Biafra, though perhaps it had. The reason is that the Indian Army beat that of Pakistan. Biafra, having no such ally, died.

The fear or threat of secession is a double-edged weapon for minorities. On the one hand, it may secure (I am not speaking now of secession itself but of a different matter: the fear or threat of it — which is much more widespread, much more impalpably and generally present, than actual examples of secession) advantages for the minority, making a majority more anxious to conciliate them lest worse befall. On the other hand, the fear it inspires may goad the majority to particularly harsh and oppressive action. There may be a cyclical alternation of these different reactions over longer or shorter periods, like the alternations of coercion and conciliation in nineteenth-century Ireland, or the oscillations in recent British policy in Northern Ireland. Finally, a population which is not in itself secessionist and which is even fairly far gone in one form or another of integration can harbour militant secessionist elements, and can regard these with the most varied and fluctuating emotions. I think here it is very important not to hypostatise monolithic minorities; they do not work like that: there is a lot of variation within them and a lot of change in those variations. Minorities can look at their militant secessionist elements, which claim to be their political vanguard, with such emotions as these: admiration, sympathy, apprehension, anxiety, guilt, fear, hatred (and I am here speaking of fear and hatred not by the minority of the majority, but fear and hatred by members of a minority of people who are claiming to be emancipating that minority). These emotions take changing patterns in response both to the activities of the militants themselves and to whatever forms of coercion or conciliation the majority is trying and with what success — all in a great flux in potential secession situations for long periods.

Minorities are in fact often divided as to what rights they really want, or what they think they want. Even individual members of such minorities are often divided within themselves about this, and change in their mood from year to year or month to month, or even at different times of the day; in the one person one can observe the most extraordinary fluctuations of ideas about what the solution is.

A partly integrated society forces versatility in role-playing in an unusual degree on minority members. I have observed in far away countries, and perhaps nearer at home, certain minority people playing one role in the presence of local majority people, a second role equally artificial in the presence of more extreme members of their own minority, and a third role, more naturally, with their own friends, all minority people but none of them aggressively minoritarian. That is a point too: minorities are not being minorities all the time; they are not constantly thinking of themselves as minorities; on the whole they only think of themselves as minorities when they are forced so to think of themselves by the definitions of majorities or ruling groups.

In the first context these people sounded like social integrationists; in the second they behaved as if they might be at heart secessionists; and in the third they showed themselves to be on the whole economic integrationists, with not much more taste for social integration in the full sense than for secession. But their conviction in the various roles could vary according to mood, the previous day's news, or even the rumours of the day itself.

In certain circumstances, minorities can find rights thrust on them which they have not so much been actually looking for as sounding as if they were looking for. Again there is an escalating factor in the rhetoric of minorities. People represented as spokesmen of minorities can often feel (sometimes consciously think, more often feel) that the more they look for, the more extreme they sound, the more they will get, without necessarily wanting the most extreme thing, such as total independence, that they sometimes look for. They may think that this is the way of getting a certain amount of control over local government; to say 'We must have immediate independence now, or else . . .', is a bargaining position. But what they intend as a bargaining position may be taken as a definitive statement by others, and they may even get locked into it by more extreme elements in their own minority.

Fourthly, there are minorities which are so placed that neither social or economic integration nor secession seems relevant to them. Thus the Crimean Tatars, it seems, neither wished to be integrated in Kazakhstan where they do not wish to be in the first place, nor to secede with any part of Kazakhstan. They just want to be allowed to return to their Crimean home. The Ugandan Asians just wanted to get out. They did not always want that; they wanted other things. But now they want to get out anywhere, with their lives, their families, with anything that they are allowed to carry. This is of course the last right, or almost the last right of a minority.

But these are extreme cases. For most it is the question of one or other form of integration, or a blend of the two, or much more rarely, of contemplated secession, independence. The last is not likely to be undertaken seriously by any sizeable body of people, except as a result of a total or at least major breakdown in an integration process.

One approach to the problem which has much to recommend it — indeed I am rather beginning to come round to it — is that it is wrong to speak of minority rights or majority rights. Rights are best thought of as inherent in each human being, irrespective of what kind of cultural grouping he or she may belong to.

Those who hold this point of view are likely to point out that the culture of a group (and when we are speaking of minorities we are always speaking of groups) may include systematic violations of basic human rights. When we are told to respect the cultures of groups we are being told to respect things which may include for example the Hindu caste system, the treatment of women in Islam and a number of other cultures, female circumcision in certain cultures, ostracism of twins, for example, in others, and so on. To speak in terms of group rights — as we do of course when we speak of minority rights at all times — may involve connivance in actual denial of rights to stigmatised members of the groups in question.

I would not lightly dismiss that argument. I think there is a great deal of force in it, and it is reflected perhaps to a rather surprising extent in such a document as the Universal Declaration of Human Rights, which always prefers to speak of rights inherent in individual human beings and *not* of group rights. In general at the United Nations, this is the approach that has been favoured, nor is there much difference between the various blocs or between developed and underdeveloped, about this matter — on the whole, 'developed' being more sympathetic to group rights than 'underdeveloped' are. This may seem surprising for more than one reason. The language of the document which people of so many cultures *appear* to find acceptable is clearly the product of one special culture, that of Western Europe including the Europeans of North America. More than that, it has been powerfully argued by people from the Third World — some people — that this generalised and abstract concern with human rights as defined by Europeans became an instrument, consciously or unconsciously applied, for the disruption of other people's cultures.

Beneath all their ultra-Third World rhetoric, most of the educated Third-World intellectuals who represent their underdeveloped countries at the United Nations and other international bodies, are the products of their coloniser's educational systems. These have no difficulty — I am talking here all the time about this question of group rights or individual rights — about the Universal Declaration, because they were brought up on the Declaration des Droits de l'Homme or its Anglo-Saxon equivalents. Any one of them would think it derogatory to their country's status were someone to suggest he might be unwilling to sign such a document, even though he might know that no such rights were in fact recognised by his own government in its daily relations with the citizens. And there of course, in some cases, he would say: 'The best thing I can do to bring about these rights is to get my government at least to sign this document so that I can then say to them, "Well, why don't you honour this?"' And this is quite sincerely put. Even where he signs in a more cynical spirit, he is not necessarily more

hypocritical tham some of his eighteenth-century predecessors,
the *philosophes*, who (like Voltaire) were not above a flutter in the
slave trade, or the slave-owners who signed the Declaration of
Independence. Universal Declarations tend to be professed with
mental reservations, sometimes unconscious, 'not for slaves', 'not
for savages', 'not for "those" people'. Sometimes the language
has helped. A Japanese, for example, could sign a declaration
setting out the rights of people without having to think at all about
the position of the outcastes in his own society, since the word for
those outcastes in his language is *hinin*, non-people. And I have
on countless occasions heard persons who were by no means
Japanese use the word 'people' in contexts where the Japanese
distinction was clearly implied.

As a matter of experience I have found — and I had to concern
myself at the U.N. with problems like that of Tibet or South
Tyrol, for example — that people who are all in favour of human
rights generally speaking are very likely to sit up and look
suspicious where there is any question of *minority* rights. Human
rights is a pleasing abstraction impregnated with our notion of
our own benevolence. But *minority rights* evoke a sudden sharp
picture of 'that lot' with their regrettable habits, extravagant
claims, ridiculous complaints, and suspect intentions. Special
rights for *them*? Not likely. Governments are representative, of
course, either of majorities or more often of ruling minorities
which of course do not think of themselves as minorities ever. It is
therefore unlikely that an international association on the scale of
the United Nations will promulgate an effective code giving
specific protection to minorities. The United Nations has
attempted from time to time to cope with this problem in a
gingerly way, but has flinched away from it. More limited bodies
like the Council of Europe, representing countries which are
more secure from secession threats, have been able to make some
progress, but the countries most affected by minority problems
and where minorities themselves have the most acute problem,
are not anxious to enter this area of discussion.

Should a private body, the Minority Rights Group for example,
attempt to draw up such a code? That would be a most difficult
task. I have tried to indicate some of the difficulties, and I am not
at all sure that its utility would be proportionate to its difficulty.
The leverage applicable to governments through their adherence
or putative adherence to the Universal Declaration is not much

(indeed it is pitiably little) but it is something. The leverage applicable through a code not accepted by governments and — almost by definition — not acceptable to them, would be likely to be nil; it might even be counter-productive.

Despite its defects, and I have tried to indicate some of them, I believe that on the whole the universalist approach, based on rights inherent in each individual being, remains the most hopeful one. We ought not, after all, to idealise minorities or to forget that today's underdog may be tomorrow's power-crazed bully. Or that certain custodians of minority cultures, and certain vehement exponents of minority political rights, may already be playing that role in their own little community. In these conditions, we ought in effect, I suggest, to be saying to governments something like this: 'We seek no special rights for minorities, your ones or any other ones. Members of minority groups should have the same human rights as members of majorities, no less and not necessarily any more for the moment than those set out in the Universal Declaration to which you subscribe. But we have evidence that shows that members of such and such a minority are being denied these rights under your government. Unless you set about correcting this situation, we shall have to publish this evidence with inevitably undesirable results for your country's reputation and prospects.'

Our most pressing concern should now perhaps be not to define what rights minorities should have, but to find what techniques are most appropriate for conveying to governments the message that decency in relation to minorities is a quality helpful to any country in its international relations.

Introduction

These brief summaries of the character and circumstances of some fifty minorities have been gathered by the Minority Rights Group to help further the increasing awareness of how, and more importantly of whom, the world is composed. To study minorities is not merely to count numbers nor to review isolated static societies, nor necessarily to assess disadvantage. It is to describe human beings relative to others: each possessing all variety of human reason and dynamic, perversity and weakness, within the boundaries and constitutional instruments of the modern nation-state. And this in relation to history, religion and myth, to ideology and international perspectives of power and peace, as well as to the forces of nature and physical location. The diversity of human type, culture, credo and language is astonishing; no nation-state is homogeneous.

This is only the first volume of what, it is hoped, will eventually be a complete world directory of minorities in conjunction with, and complementary to, the series of fuller Reports published by the Minority Rights Group. It has been necessary to be selective, but each entry attempts to describe the basic facts on a minority group in its national and international context. Not all are victims of direct oppression or of exploitation — although there are repeated instances of how easy it is to exploit the new dazed immigrant, the nomad whose close society is crumbling, or the people of the peripheries whose land is suddenly known to be mineral-rich. Some, indeed, are heirs to their own intransigence or of historical privilege in course of readjustment; some have been courted, used and deserted by foreign powers, while others are potential victims. Although each entry expresses the personal view and reflects the individual approach of its author, I hope that they will, as a whole, not only inform but give some insight both into the variety of current minority problems and — perhaps indirectly — into the nature of conflict and identity, of nationalism and constitutional justice. It cannot escape notice that, although these summaries represent the status of whole societies, in practice the lives and aspirations of their women are, in almost every case, comparatively more constricted and disadvantaged by custom, convention and circumstance.

I should like to thank all the authors: journalists, scholars and individuals of goodwill all over the world, many of whom contributed their talents voluntarily, as do so many of the friends of MRG — and in particular Alexander Kirby, John Gaisford, Peter Sherwin and Pam Cox who helped with the toils of editing and preparing the manuscript. I hope that successor volumes will be as fortunate, and I invite contributions to this continuous task, which should be sent to me at MRG. I am also grateful for the support and guidance of the Director of MRG, Ben Whitaker, to its Secretary Pat Oakley and my predecessor, Beverley Lang, and to my husband, Roy, and my family whose consequent awareness of human geography and predicament will, I hope, one day make its own contribution.

Georgina Ashworth

Minority Rights Group
36 Craven Street
London WC2N 5NG
England

1 The Adivasis: The 'Scheduled Tribes' of India

By a constitutional order in 1950, the President of India declared 212 tribes in the country to be the 'Scheduled Tribes'. These 38 million people account for 6.7% of the national population according to the 1971 census. The term *adivasis* (literally 'the original inhabitants') generally used to describe these tribes, is apt. They have a much longer history of settlement in the Indian sub-continent than the latter-day Indo-Aryan tribes. The gradual ascendancy of the Aryan colonizers in the sub-continent, which began in 1500 BC, caused these tribes to be pushed into the uncongenial environment of hilly forests. For centuries, often cut off from outside influences, they existed on a subsistence economy, gathering fruit and engaging in shift cultivation. These tribes of Mongoloid, Australoid or Dravidian stock are to be found chiefly in three zones: north-eastern, central, and southern. The main tribes in the north-east are Nagas, Mizos, Tripuris, Luchais, Garos, Khasis, Meiteis, Mikir, Kukis, Riangs; those in the central region — which extends from the Orissa-West Bengal border in the east to Gujarat in the west — are Santals, Oraons, Mundas, Baigas, Murias, Khonds, Kharias, Hos, Bhils, and Gonds. And the major tribes in the south are Girijans, Paniyans, Uralys, and Kadans.

On the eve of independence, most of the tribals stood outside the mainstream of Hindu dominated Indian society. The life of the tribals in the jungle-covered southern Bihar-western Orissa region, for instance, had not been disturbed until the latter half of the sixteenth century, when the Mughal rulers first penetrated these forests, and it was only after the arrival of the British that *adivasi* life was materially affected by the intrusion of the non-adivasis. British rule brought money, government officials and moneylenders into the tribal areas, causing the gradual encroachment of *adivasi* land by outsiders. Christian

1

missions began to educate the *adivasis* as well as to proselytize.

Since 1947, political, social, educational and industrial developments have brought about some changes, particularly in the mineral-rich region of West Bengal–southern Bihar–western Orissa, which is being commercially exploited. This has accelerated the loss of *adivasi* ancestral land to non-adivasis for meagre sums, leaving great numbers rootless and unskilled.

Laws designed to halt these transfers of the tribal lands have, by and large, proved ineffective. On the other hand, governmental policies of helping 'the weaker sections of society' in education, civil service and legislatures have had some success. Special encouragement is given to tribal parents to educate their children, yet the historic lag is so wide that the current literacy rate among the Scheduled Tribes varies from one-sixth the national average in the State of Andhra Pradesh to one-third the national average in the State of Kerala. The policy of reserving seats in legislatures and jobs in civil service has been more successful. Of the 524 seats in the lower house of the national Parliament, 42 are reserved for the Scheduled Tribes; and of the 3,864 seats in various State and other legislative assemblies, 329 are so reserved. In civil service, 7½% of the jobs are reserved for them.

This has not banished the deeply rooted prejudice against the Scheduled Tribes, particularly among the caste Hindus, the largest and most powerful section of society. To them, the *adivasis* are 'junglis' (literally, forest-dwellers), uncivilized, irreligious and innately inferior. Social intercourse between tribals and caste Hindus is rare.

The communal goals of the tribals, and the methods used to achieve them have been varied. In the north-eastern areas of Nagaland and Mizoram, the tribals have been known to back a demand for total independence, and have used violent means to try to achieve it. Elsewhere, as in southern Bihar, they have tended to support a party — such as the Jharkhand Party — which calls for the creation of a State with a tribal majority. In other parts of the country, the tribals are too widely and thinly spread out to pursue any such aim.

The social and other form of integration of tribals into the mainstream of Indian society depends, in a general sense, on the ability of the present socio-economic system to engender a

steadily increasing Gross National Product, and a more equitable
way of distributing income and wealth than is the case now.

Dilip Hiro

SELECT BIBLIOGRAPHY

Ehrenfels, U.R., *The Kadar of Cochin,* University of Madras,
Madras, 1952
Fuchs, S., *The Gond and Bhumia of Eastern Mandla,* Asia Publishing
House, New York, 1960
Majumdar, D.N., *The Affairs of a Tribe: A Study in Tribal
Dynamics,* University Publishers, Lucknow, 1950
Maxwell, N., *India and the Nagas,* Minority Rights Group.
London, 1973
Nath, Y.V.S., *Bhils of Ratanmal,* University of Baroda, Baroda,
1960
Orans, M., *The Santhels,* Wayne State University Press, Detroit,
1964
Sachidananda, *Cultural Change in Tribal Bihar,* Bookland Private,
Bombay, 1964.
*Twenty-Second Report of the Commissioner for Scheduled Castes and
Scheduled Tribes, 1972–73,* Publications Division, Ministry of
Information and Broadcasting, Government of India, New Delhi
Verrier, E., *A Philosophy for North East Frontier Agency,* North East
Frontier Agency, Shillong, 1959

2   The Afars and The Issas

When the French pull out of Djibouti it will mark the end of an
era. For the *Territoire Francaise des Afars et des Issas* or TFAI,
better known by the name of its capital, Djibouti, is Europe's last
colony in Africa. This hot and desolate land has little economic
value. Without the French presence its people would have one of
the lowest *per capita* incomes in the world. Its importance has
always stemmed from its strategic location commanding the
Bab-al-Mandeb Straits at the outlet of the Red Sea.

The TFAI is an enclave surrounding the Bay of Tadjoura near the mouth of the Red Sea. At 23,000 sq.km. (8,800 sq.ml.) it is little bigger than Wales, has perhaps the hottest climate in Africa and is almost entirely desert with barren volcanic hills, dry wadis, desolate lava fields, and a gravel coastal plain with sparse thorn scrub vegetation. The indigenous population of about 200,000 has 62,000 Issas, who are a Somali people, and 82,000 Afars, who are the same as the neighbouring Ethiopian Danakils. Both are hamitic peoples and staunchly Muslim, and it is hard for a foreigner to tell them apart. About two-thirds of the population are settled; the rest roam across the borders of either Ethiopia or Somalia in search of grazing for their camels and goats. Small minority groups of Arabic and Amharic speaking poeple live in the capital and coastal towns together with several thousand civilian French expatriates and a military garrison of variable strength, estimated to have reached 20,000 men during the more serious internal disorders of recent years and including the famous Foreign Legion.

France negotiated a treaty with the principal Issa sultan in the region in 1862 and this led to the establishment of a small naval base at Obock. The territory was only formally annexed and became French Somaliland following the Conference of Berlin in 1884 which accelerated the 'scramble for Africa'. Construction of a deep water port and town at Djibouti began soon after and the capital was transferred there from Obock in 1892. The significance of Djibouti was enhanced with the construction by French engineers of a railway from the port to Addis Ababa.

Following severe riots during a visit by General de Gaulle in 1966, a referendum on independence was held in March 1967, and produced a majority for French rule, although this result was marred by widespread allegations of electoral malpractices. French Somaliland was then renamed the TFAI, some say to emphasise the existence of two disparate population groups. The local Chamber of Deputies was expanded, but France, represented by a High Commissioner, retained complete control of defence, foreign policy, security and finance. A deputy and a senator from the TFAI were appointed to attend Parliament in Paris.

Opposition to French rule continued, fuelled by Somali interest in the Issas' cause, and perhaps a Greater Somalia, and internationally growing pressures for decolonisation. The only official opposition party represented in the local assembly was the Afar-dominated *Ligue Populaire Africaine pour l'Independence* (LPAI). The much more militant and, as far as the French were concerned, illegal, *Front pour la Liberation de la Cote Somali* (or FLCS), is based in Somalia; and the *Movement pour la Liberation de Djiboutie* (MLD) based in Ethiopia.

The people of the TFAI were consulted further with two elections held during 1973 in which the ruling party under the Chief Minister, Ali Aref Borhan, was returned by an adequate but reduced majority on a platform for continuing ties with France. However, again there were widespread complaints of serious electoral malpractice. Allegations included complaints that thousands of Issas were deported from the TFAI immediately before the election, troops from the large French garrison were allowed to participate, that certain opposition candidates were arbitrarily disqualified, that the rural vote was largely in the hands of a few chiefs with tribal 'card votes', and worst of all, that the voting operation was under the questionable control of Ali Aref's ruling party. A counter-argument maintained that many Issas were Somali nationals, residing illegally in the shanty towns round Djibouti, there to swell the FLCS vote. The city is surrounded by a cordon of barbed wire 11 km. (7 ml.) long, known locally as *'le barrage'* and said to be mined.

Tension continued with sporadic outbursts of violence between the TFAI government and the Somalis, and increasingly the French. The opposition LPAI accused Ali Aref's ruling party of inciting Afar elements against the Issa community to lend substance to French allegations that the two peoples cannot co-exist. The new Ethiopian government, meeting armed resistance to the land reform programme from its own Afars, whose sultan has suggested a greater Afaria, now supported the territorial integrity of the TFAI, while the Somali government abrogated the use of force, but called for self-determination within the territory. In December 1975 the UN General Assembly, following the Trusteeship Council, called for immediate and unconditional independence. The French response was to declare the resolution contrary to the non-intervention clauses of the Charter, but in February 1976 began negotiations towards independence, to be guaranteed by the OAU, and promised another referendum before the end of the year. In July Ali Aref resigned as Prime Minister feeling he had lost the confidence of both France and the majority, many of his supporters having gradually shifted to the LPAI, or to support Senator Barkhat. The new government — pledged to independence early in 1977, the detribalisation of political life, and the recasting of the electoral roll and reform of nationality laws — is composed of 6 Issas and 4 Afars. A government of independence will face severe economic problems maintaining an infrastructure that is now heavily dependent on French subsidies and aid. The economy is based primarily on port and railway revenues from Ethiopia, fattened by the spending power of the wealthy expatriate community and large garrison.

So the main reason for the continuing French presence was Djibouti's strategic importance as a naval base. France's aspirations to maintain a credible global independent defence, led to an expansion of Djibouti's naval facilities, particularly since the French navy vacated its former base on Madagascar. No doubt the re-opening of the Suez Canal coupled with increased Soviet naval activity in the region (including their use of port facilities in Somalia, North and South Yemen), together with the uncertainties over what will happen in the vacuum left after France withdraws will have attracted the attention of the U.S. government, already heavily committed to assisting the present government in Ethiopia.

The significance of the railway line and road from Djibouti to Addis Ababa, now threatened by the little known fighting in the Aissata-Afar-area of Wollo province in Ethiopia, will not therefore be lost on the Americans. Only time will show whether Afars and Issas can live in peace together in Djibouti, but the circumstances of the French withdrawal, of the American presence nearby, and of Somali nationalism, with Soviet influence, will be factors with which they will have to contend.

Peter Fraenkel

SELECT BIBLIOGRAPHY

Bell, J.B., Jnr., *The Horn of Africa — Strategic Magnet in the 70s*, Crane Russell, New York, 1973
Farer, T.J., *War Clouds on the Horn of Africa: A Crisis for Detente*, Carnegie Endowment for International Peace, Washington, 1976
Fraenkel, Peter, 'The French Territory of the Afars and Issas', *Geographical Magazine*, April 1976

3 The Ahmadis of Pakistan

In September 1974 the Ahmadiyya community was declared 'non-Moslem' according to the Constitution of Pakistan by both houses of the National Assembly. The struggle by certain factions to bring about this declaration has continued since Partition, and its accomplishment is due less to religion than to other pressures.

Hard-working, educated, tightly-knit and relatively few in number — estimates vary between half and five million out of a total population of 65 million — the Ahmadi community have always played a prominent part in industry and commerce, military, civil and diplomatic service, largely by supporting the government of the day, whether civil or military.

The founder of the sect, Mirza Ghirlam Ahmad (1839–1908) claimed prophetic status as the *Mahdi*, or Messiah, in succession to Mohammed, Jesus Christ and Krishna, and the authority to reinterpret the Koran in modern terms. Of the five basic principles of Islam — prayer five times a day; Ramadan or thirty days fasting; the Haj, or pilgrimage to Mecca; giving alms to the poor; the Jihad, or Holy War against non-believers — he rejected the last. Socially progressive and strongly proseletysing, the Ahmadiyya sect originated in Qadiani in the Punjab, and Ahmadis were often employed in the Civil Service by the British which, with their rejection of the Jihad, rendered them politically quiescent during the struggle for Independence, and Partition (after which Qadiani Ahmadis crossed the border from the Indian Punjab to West Pakistan). With the lack of ethnic unity, common language and uniform culture in Pakistan, it was regarded as essential to forge a strong Islamic (Sunni) constitution in the interests of political unity and nationhood. In May 1949, the *Ahrar* (one of several regional conservative politico-religious parties) first called for the Ahmadis to be declared non-Moslem; and the *Ulama* (a faction of religious leaders hoping to base the Constitution and its interpretation on

7

Seventh Century Islam) sought to influence the 'Basic Principles
(of Islam) Committee', the all-Moslem Parties Congress, and the
Government on the same grounds, with constitutional
suggestions on the composition of the Courts under Islamic law as
well as the educational structure, thus excluding any modernist
influence. The Foreign Minister, Sir Mohammed Zarullah Khan,
was an Ahmadi, and it was felt that, apart from their neutral role
at independence, the Ahmadis occupied a position and influence
in society disproportionate to their numbers.

Unrest continued, culminating in riots in Lahore, capital of the
Punjab, in 1953. The Munir Report, examining the causes of
their riots, later found that certain newspapers had been paid by
the conservative politico-religious parties to incite hatred and
violence against the Ahmadi community. Sir Zarullah Khan, and
later the Prime Minister, had been forced to resign this time, but
the report led to the weakening of the anti-Ahmadi groups, and
to relative peace for the Ahmadi community over the next decade
of political change — and external conflict with India.

In the 1970 elections the Ahmadi community lent support to
President Bhutto, and were returned to the National Assembly
and the Provincial Assembly of the Punjab in large numbers. It
has become politic again, however, to emphasise the common
religion of Pakistan: since the separation of Bangladesh from
Pakistan, and with the growing threat of separatism from the
Baluchis in the South West and Pathans in the North, the struggle
for popular support for any government has become more
difficult. The need to retain supplies of oil by friendship with
co-religionists in the Middle East rendered it necessary to
acquiesce in the Islamic States Conference's pronunciation in
March 1974 at Jeddah that the Ahmadi were non-Moslem and
could no longer take part in the Haj (the previous Islamic
conference had been at Lahore, presumably to indicate
orthodoxy). The Ahmadis position on the Jihad, potentially
undermining anti-Israeli solidarity, also probably played some
part in this decision.

After increasing sectarian riots in April and May 1974 (seven
mosques were burnt, 500 shops and houses looted, 2000 people
made homeless, with 42 killed, of whom 27 were Ahmadis)
President Bhutto yielded on 13th June to the opposition parties'
demands that the position of the Ahmadis be re-examined. A
General Strike, on 14th June, compounded this decision and

Bhutto, who had enforced strict censorship and ordered arrests under the Defence of Pakistan Rules for 'publishing objectionable . . . and sectarian material', agreed to his Pakistan People's Party receiving a free vote on this issue in the National Assembly, before referring it to the Council of Islamic Ideology. But on 30th June the Assembly announced it would convene itself into a special committee, with the Speaker as Chairman, to determine the 'status of persons who did not believe Mohammed was the only prophet'.

The National Assembly received evidence in camera, and on 7th September adopted a constitutional amendment that 'persons not believing in the absolute and unqualified finality of the prophethood of Mohammed' were not Moslems for the purpose of the Constitution or Law. Special seats should be reserved for the Ahmadis in the Provincial Assemblies thus classifying them with the Christians, Hindus, Sikhs, Buddhists, Parsees and members of the non-scheduled castes, guaranteed protection by law, but not eligible to become President or Prime Minister (or to marry Moslems). In addition, a resolution was adopted stipulating that any Moslem 'professing, practising or propagating against the finality of the prophethood of Mohammed' would be punished under the penal code.

The Ahmadis continue to regard themselves as faithful followers of Islam and the loss of life and their social and influential position is probably of equal or less importance to them than the loss of their religious status.

Georgina Ashworth

Select Bibliography

Callard, K., *Pakistan Politics,* Allen and Unwin, London, 1957
Wheeler, R.S., *The Politics of Pakistan — A Constitutional Quest,* Cornell University Press, Ithaca N.Y., 1970

4 The Anglo-Indians of India

The quarter-million strong Anglo-Indian community is the smallest officially recognised minority in India. Article 366(2) of the Indian Constitution of 1950 defines an Anglo-Indian as 'a person whose father or any of whose male progenitors in the male line is or was of European descent but who is domiciled within the territory of India and is or was born within such territory of parents habitually resident therein and not established there for temporary purposes only'.

The Anglo-Indian community originated soon after 1639 — the year when the British East India Company founded a settlement in Madras. The commmunity identified itself with, and was accepted by, the British and enjoyed the status and privilege of the ruling elite. This continued until 1791, when the British East India Company decided to exclude persons of Indian extraction from positions of authority in the civil, military, and marine services of the Company. But when Indian soldiers and others rebelled against the British in 1857, and a series of bloody battles ensued, the Anglo-Indians sided with the British. The British government, which assumed direct responsibility for the administration of India in 1858, consequently initiated a policy of patronage towards the Anglo-Indians. It raised a regiment of Anglo-Indians, stationed in Bengal.

The Anglo-Indians actively supported the war effort during World War I, serving in the strategic services of Railways, Post and Telegraph, and Customs in large numbers. In 1919 the community was given one reserved seat in the Central Legislative Assembly in Delhi, and was united behind the All India Anglo-Indian and Domiciled European Association, formed in 1926, as a result of the merger of two separate organisations. They joined the Auxiliary Force, India's second line of defence after the first war, so that on the eve of World War II, two-thirds of the 29,000 strong Auxiliary Force consisted of Anglo-Indians, the rest being 'Domiciled Europeans'. During the war, the Anglo-Indians identified themselves wholeheartedly with the British, while the nationalist Congress Party agitated for immediate independence as a condition for co-operation with the British government.

On the eve of departure of the British from India, the Anglo-Indians found themselves in an invidious situation — caught between the European attitude of superiority towards Indian and the Anglo-Indian alike, and the Indian mistrust of them, due to their aloofness and their western orientated culture. The history taught in their schools had been British, and they had served the colonial government. Now that they had to be integrated fully into an independent India, seats were reserved for the Anglo-Indians in legislatures. Article 331 of the Constitution states 'The President may, if he is of the opinion that the Anglo-Indian community is not adequately represented in the House of the People, nominate not more than two members of that community to the House of the People', in practice, one Anglo-Indian gets nominated to this House of 524 members. A similar provision is made in State legislatures. Two other articles stipulated reservation of posts for the Anglo-Indians in the Railways, Post and Telegraph, and Customs, and financial assistance to the Anglo-Indian educational institutions for the following twenty years. However, the Anglo-Indian efforts to have English, their mother-tongue, classified as an Indian language and included in the Constitution, proved unsuccessful.

The community went through a difficult period of adjustment during the first decade of independence. Many of its members migrated to Britain and Australia. By now, however, the community has found its niche in the contemporary Indian society. The Anglo-Indians continue to serve, in large numbers, those departments of the government which they have traditionally done — Defence Forces, Railways, Post and Telegraph, and Customs — and are largely accepted in the polyglot society of urban India. Ironic though it may seem, the 100% literate and urbanised Anglo-Indian community, spread throughout the country, is probably the only group today that can truly be called 'All Indian'.

Dilip Hiro

SELECT BIBLIOGRAPHY

Anthony, F., *Britain's Betrayal in India: The Story of the Anglo-Indian Community,* Allied Publishers, Bombay, 1969
Dover, C., *Half Caste,* Secker and Warburg, London, 1937
Maher, R., *These are the Anglo-Indians,* Swallow Press, Calcutta, 1962
Stark, H.A., *Call of the Blood,* British Burma Press, Rangoon, 1932
Wallace, K., *Brave New Anglo-India,* Modern Art Press, Calcutta, 1935

5 The Azores and Madeira Islanders

The nine Azores islands lie 1300–1800 kms. west of Lisbon and 2100 kms. from Newfoundland; the two Madeira islands are 850 kms. from Lisbon and 580 kms. from the coast of Morocco. The archipelagos were discovered by Europeans in 1351 and settled by the Portuguese in the next century. The union of the Iberian crowns, 1580–1640, brought Spanish immigration; the archipelagos also have Flemish, British and African blood. The Azores population has hardly risen since 1900, due to emigration, with a 12% (38,000) decrease during 1960–70; there are an estimated 500,000 emigrés in America. Madeira's population rose until 1960 but dropped 6% (15,000) in the next decade. The Azores' inhabitants are in the main peasants working for large landowners, each group strongly Catholic; Madeira has particularly difficult farming conditions, with a dense rural population of 316 persons per sq.km. (126 per sq.km. in the Azores).

	Populations 1970	%	Emigration 1974	%	% of population
Azores	290,000	3	12,400	29	4
Madeira	253,000	3	4,400	10	1.7
Portugal (including islands)	8,660,000	100	43,400	100	.5

	% to Canada	% to U.S.	% to Venezuela	% to Brazil	% to France	% to U.K.	% to elsewhere
Azores	63	35	1	—	—	—	—
Madeira	6	6	44	4	10	12	18
Portugal (including islands)	26	22	6	2	24	2	18

The table shows both that emigration is much higher from the islands than from the Peninsula and also that it follows different patterns from that of the mainland.

The Azores see Portugal as a liability. Contrastingly, much income is derived from U.S. tourism and the air-base of Lajes on Terceira and, through the emigrés and their remittances, there is much sympathy for the U.S. and its materially attractive way of life. The spread of communism on the mainland was resented in the Azores, with fear for its consequences; the Communist Party received only 2% of the Azores' votes at the Constituent Assembly elections of April 1975. The traditional smouldering grievances, such as the farmers' complaints of mainland-oriented agricultural legislation, were now set alight and independence was demanded for the islands. The possibility was made the more feasible by the sight of Lisbon relinquishing the African colonies.

The movement was led by the 'Azorean Liberation Front', or FLA. The offices of the Communist Party and other associated groups ('Movement of the Socialist left', 'Portuguese Democratic Movement — Democratic Electoral Committee') were systematically attacked throughout the islands, the last being forced to close in August 1975. A second tactic was to bring about the resignation of the civil governors of the islands, together with that of communists holding posts in the farming co-operatives. This led, in August, to the surrender of internal administration by the Portuguese government to six islanders chosen by the Socialist and Popular Democratic parties. This was promised to be leading to self-government but since then the FLA, threatening to renew the violence, has claimed that no further steps were being taken in this direction. The FLA announced the formation of a 'provisional and clandestine Government of the Democratic Republic of the Azores'. The movement's stated aims are:

1. Independence; to end political, economic, social and cultural domination by peninsula Portugal, with full U.N. status
2. Elections leading to a western-style democracy
3. The rapid raising of living standards, with better use of human and material resources
4. Respect for the traditions of the islanders.

Outside the Azores, the campaign derives strong moral and financial aid from the islanders in America; a recent law allows

Portugal emigres to vote in elections. Political support is strongest amongst the liberal Popular Democratic Party, with the majority vote in the islands at the last election, and from the right-wing Democratic Social Centre; their policy is unpopular on the mainland, where the Azores' independence claim is not seen in the same light as those of the African colonies. The Socialist Party has, on the other hand, adopted a manifesto designed to give devolution and increased wealth without separation from the Peninsula. It hopes that at the next election it will get the support of those afraid of the results of full independence and of the opening thus created for the U.S., which is interested in ensuring the stability of the strategically-placed archipelago.

In 1975 Madeira underwent much the same internal evolution as did the Azores. Communism in Lisbon coupled with long-standing island grievances led to an independence demand, expressed by the 'Madiera Archipelago Liberation Front' or FLAMA. This carried out bomb attacks and attempted to bring about the removal of the civil governor. A 'provisional government' was announced in August 1975. The FLAMA has suggested federation with the Azores and the Canaries, though the MPAIAC's principles do not seem compatible with those of the Portuguese movements. In Madeira too the Popular Democratic Party supports the independence claim and has the majority vote. Several other separatist groups have been formed in Madeira; the 'Independence for Madeira Movement' (IDM), the 'Madeira Liberation Army' (ELMA), and the 'Revolutionary Brigade for the Independence of Madiera' (BRIMA).

The general ethnic similarity of the Madeiras' population to that of the Peninsula probably shows that — as in the Azores but less so in the Canaries, with their claim to a Berber element — the independence demand is the island workers' expression of the discontent felt by the poorer people throughout Portugal. Their problems are heightened by the islands' peculiar conditions and their remoteness from the centralised authority. It seems that, compared to the Azores, Madeira is less far advanced along the road to independence.

John Mercer

6 The Baluchis of Pakistan

The 1.3 million Baluchi speakers form 2% of the population of Pakistan (64.9 million, according to the 1972 census). Of these, nearly a million live in Baluchistan, where they form 40% of the province's inhabitants. The Baluchi tribes and their kinsmen, the Brahui-speaking tribes — who make their living principally as herdsmen of sheep and farmers — are to be found mainly in the central, southern, and eastern parts of Baluchistan, a vast, remote, mountainous province, with a long and chequered history. Until the advance of the Arab armies into the area in the seventh century, it was part of Iran. During the eleventh century, the nomadic Baluchi tribes — whose origins can be traced back to their ancient Babylonian homeland of Aleppo, Syria — began to arrive in the region, and by the end of the fifteenth century inhabited most of the province. Baluchistan had by then been incorporated into the Mughal empire of India. But when Nasir Khan Baloch of Kalat welded together various feudal states in 1730, he aligned himself with the ruler of Iran. After his death, however, the province broke up into small principalities once again.

The ruler of Kalat accepted British suzerainty in 1854, and during the next few decades, the other potentates in the region followed suit, so that by 1891 the British government had consolidated its rule in the area, and divided it into (directly administered) British Baluchistan, tribal areas, and the princely State of Kalat. With the departure of the British in 1947, and partition of the Indian sub-continent, Baluchistan became part of Pakistan. A year later, the State of Kalat acceded to Pakistan. And in 1955, both these areas were merged, along with others, into a single unit: West Pakistan.

This arrangement continued until 1970, when Baluchistan and other former smaller provinces were re-established, and popular elections held. The National Awami Party, which campaigned

15

mainly for greater provincial autonomy, emerged as the most
popular in Baluchistan. In April 1972 — when administrative
power was transferred from the military, which had ruled
Pakistan since 1958, to civilian political parties — the National
Awami Party formed a coalition government in Baluchistan.

Chiefly because the National Awami Party and its coalition
partner were in opposition to the ruling Pakistan People's Party
in the National Assembly in Islamabad, the government in
Baluchistan was dismissed by the central authorities, and the
leaders of the National Awami Party imprisoned. This caused
popular discontent, particularly among the Baluchis and Brahuis
of the province. Many of the Baluchi students left the university
in Quetta, the provincial capital, and joined the militant tribals
operating from hideouts in the mountains, to conduct an armed
guerilla struggle against Federal authority. The central
government sent in troops, took repressive action, and succeeded
in isolating the guerillas.

These developments have brought to the fore the question of
Baluchi identity — the fate of the Baluchi language and culture.
The anomaly in Pakistan is that while Urdu is the mother-tongue
of only 8% of the people, it is the first langauge to be taught in all
schools, except where Sindhi is the mother tongue of the
students. Urdu — the language of educated Muslims of north
India, including (Pakistani) Punjab — has been ideologically
associated with Muslim nationalism and the creation of Pakistan,
while neither Punjabi (the mother-tongue of 66% of Pakistanis)
nor Pashto (the mother-tongue of 13.5% of Pakistanis) has any
written literary tradition or script.

However, the preamble to the Constitution of Pakistan states
that 'adequate provision shall be made for the minorities freely to
profess and practise their religions and develop their cultures',
and that 'adequate provision shall be made to safeguard the
legitimate interests of minorities and backward and depressed
classes'. And, in Quetta, there exists the Baluchi Academy,
dedicated to the investigation and preservation of Baluchi culture
and literary traditions of Baluchistan.

The government public education programme has had only a
marginal impact on the predominantly nomadic, pastoral, and
feudal Baluchis. This puts the community at a tremendous
disadvantage. For, the political and cultural future of the
Baluchis (and the Brahuis) depends, to a large extent, on the

speed with which the community can raise a vocal and educated class of Baluchi professionals, petty bourgeoisie and entrepreneurs.

D.K.H.

SELECT BIBLIOGRAPHY

Ahmed, F. (Ed), *Focus on Baluchistan and Pushtoon Question,* People's Publishing House, Lahore, 1975
Baluch, M.S.K., *History of Baluch Race and Baluchistan,* Author, Quetta, 1959
Dames, M.L., *The Balochi Race: A Historical and Ethnological Sketch,* OUP, London, 1904
Marri-Baloch, M.K.B., *The Balochis Through Centuries: History versus Legend,* Author, Quetta, 1964
Marri-Baloch, M.K.B., *Searchlights on Balochs and Balochistan,* Royal Book Co., Karachi, 1974

7   Bangladesh's Hindus

The proportion of Hindus in Bangladesh has been declining steadily since 1947, when the Sylhet area of Assam was merged with the eastern districts of Bengal to form East Pakistan. At that time Hindus formed 31% of the province's population of some forty-two million. Due to the migration of 3.3 million Hindus to India during the next few years, this fell to 24% in 1951, and 18.5% in 1961. Now, at roughly 10 million, they constitute only 14% of the total population of 71.32 million (1974 census).

Being at the extreme end of the Gangetic plain, the ancient tribal settlers of Bengal were left practically undisturbed by the Aryan colonisers until the time of consolidation of the Gupta empire in the fifth century. This marked the introduction of Brahmin-dominated Hinduism into the region. The conquering Brahmin and other upper castes treated the indigenous population as inferior and low caste; and the latter showed their resentment by lending support to movements that challenged the

supremacy of Brahmins. They leaned towards casteless
Buddhism during the rule of Buddhist Pala kings, which lasted
from the eighth to the twelfth century. When the Afghans and
Mughals later established their rule in Bengal and Islam became
the state religion, many of the low castes and outcastes adopted
Islam. By the time the British arrived in the mid-eighteenth
century, a little over half of the Bengali population was Muslim.
Two centuries later when the British left, the two communities in
Bengal were almost equal in size.

The partition of Bengal in 1947 left six million Muslims in the
Indian State of West Bengal and thirteen million Hindus in East
Pakistan. The inter-religious violence that preceded partition,
and continued intermittently during the next few years, was not
considered serious enough by the governments of India and
Pakistan to warrant an official exchange of population as had
been done in the Punjab. The existence of Hindus in East
Pakistan was reflected in the eighty-member strong Constituent
Assembly of Pakistan: of the forty-four members from East
Pakistan, thirteen were Hindus. In the first general election to the
legislature of East Pakistan in 1954, almost all of the 72 seats
reserved for the minorities out of a total of 309, went to the
Hindus.

The Hindu members of the East Pakistan Assembly and the
Pakistani Constituent Assembly protested in vain against the
adoption of the Directive Principles of State Policy, which
included 'promotion of Islamic principles', and a statement that
'steps shall be taken to enable the Muslims of Pakistan
individually and collectively to order their lives in accordance
with the Holy Quran and *sunnat*', and the provision that the
President of the Islamic Republic of Pakistan had to be Muslim.
They also demanded the abolition of separate electoral rolls for
Muslims and non-Muslims and the stipulation that a Muslim
could only vote for a Muslim, and a non-Muslim for a
non-Muslim. This was conceded by the national government in
1957; but before elections on the basis of the joint electorate
could be held in East Pakistan, in February, 1959, the Constitution
was abrogated and a military rule imposed in the country.

The result of the general election of 1970 — in which the
Awami League, led by Sheikh Mujibur Rahman won almost all of
the seats allotted to East Pakistan — created a political impasse in
Pakistan. Although Hindus were not in the forefront of this

movement, they became the main target of persecution and repression by the (West) Pakistani troops and para-military forces stationed in the province. A large majority of the Hindus abandoned their homes and took refuge in India. War broke out between India and Pakistan as a result of which an independent Bangladesh was established, after which many Hindus returned.

A year later a republican Constitution was adopted by the country's popular representatives. 'The principles of nationalism, socialism, democracy and secularism, together with the principles derived from them ... shall constitute the fundamental principles of State policy', was a clause established under Article 8. 'The principle of secularism shall be realised by the elimination of — (a) communalism in all its forms; (b) the granting by the State of political status in favour of any religion; (c) the abuse of religion for political purposes; and (d) any discrimination against, or persecution of, persons practising a particular religion', Article 12 and Article 28 declare: 'The State shall not discriminate against any citizen on grounds only of religion, race, caste, sex or place of birth'. Article 121 states specifically that 'no special (electoral) roll shall be prepared so as to classify electors according to religion, race, caste or sex'. The practice of reserving seats for the Hindus in civil service and institutions of higher education too was discontinued.

The overall results of these policies have not been totally beneficial to the Hindus. In the general election of 1973, for instance, only 4% of the successful candidates were Hindu. The end of Sheikh Mujib's administration, and his assassination in August 1975 by a group of military officers, generally regarded as anti-Indian, has engendered feelings of insecurity among the Hindus. Resentment against the big-brotherly attitude of India towards Bangladesh, at popular and bureaucratic levels, often tends to find an expression in actions against Hindus, who are at best considered 'pro-India', and at worst, 'Indian agents'. Since the issuance of the Vested and Non-Resident Property (Administration) Ordinance of 1974, there have been complaints by many Hindus — often medium-sized landholders — that the ordinance is being harshly interpreted and executed to dispossess them of their property.

For better or worse, the fate of the Hindus in Bangladesh is intermeshed with the relationship between India and Bangladesh. Although the cordial relations that existed between the two

countries from January 1972 to August 1975 are not likely to
return, there is little chance of open war between the two
neighbours. The future of the Hindu minority in Bangladesh is
likely to remain 'grey', particularly as both India and Bangladesh,
formally committed as they are to the policy of 'secularism', are
unlikely to consider the proposition that there be an official
exchange of minority populations between Bangladesh and West
Bengal, which in 1971 had more than 8 million Muslims.

D.H.

SELECT BIBLIOGRAPHY

Ahmad, K.U., *Break-up of Pakistan,* Social Science Publishers,
London, 1972
Loshak, D., *Pakistan Crisis,* Heinemann, London, 1971
Sayeed, K.B., *Pakistan: The Formative Phase, 1857–1948,* Oxford
University Press, London, 1968
Tayyeb, A., *Pakistan: A Political Geography,* Oxford University
Press, London, 1966
Tinker, H., *India and Pakistan: A Political Analysis,* Praeger, New
York, 1963

8   The Bedouin

The Bedouin are Arab pastoral nomads who inhabit desert areas
stretching from the Western Sahara to Iran. The word Bedouin
comes from the Arabic word '*badawi*', plural '*badu*', meaning
desert dweller, and the use of this word defines the Bedouin by a
way of life that distinguishes him from other Arabs; a cultural not
a racial distinction.

Until recently the Bedouin were a substantial part of the
population, but they are now a minority in all Arab countries. For
those who remain their nomadic way of life is increasingly seen by
governments as an anachronism within the modern state. All
governments practise a policy that they hope will lead eventually
to the settlement of the Bedouin, usually by encouraging them to

become settled agriculturalists. They provide loans, agricultural machinery and technical instruction free or at low rates and set up programmes of irrigation and development aiming to bring the Bedouin into modern society with its economic benefits. But another reason is doubtless to weaken the Bedouin as an independent political element. Bedouin society is tribal; a tribe can vary in size from a few hundred to many thousands and their structure is based on geneological principles. All members see themselves as descended from one ancestry and membership is inherited through the male line (agnatically); a man's personal geneology expresses his position in the tribe and his relationships to others.

The land which the Bedouin inhabit is divided up into tribal areas in which the members have collective rights of grazing. There are also traditional circuits of migration round which the tribes move. After the rains in the winter small groups, usually composed of a core of agnatically related males, migrate in search of fresh pastures. As these pastures dry up towards the summer larger tribal groupings will congregate round oases. Migration may often take the Bedouin over tribal areas other than their own. There would either be some kind of agreement between the tribes which allowed them grazing rights or if there was no agreement there would be raiding and fighting.

Much of the earlier actions of the governments concerned was to quell continual tribal warfare. Pacification has now largely been achieved, often by making use of the Bedouin fighting tradition by employing them in the state army or police force. The National Guard in Saudi Arabia is made up of Bedouin, each military division being based on a tribe. And today the Bedouin are a recruiting ground for mercenaries all over the Middle East. Another problem for modern governments has been that tribal boundaries do not follow modern frontiers, and the circuits extend across more than one country. Since a Bedouin would define himself politically by reference to his tribe rather than to a state, this is seen as a threat to national unity. One step has been to pass laws which no longer recognise legally the tribe as a separate entity within the state, nor secondly, the tribal possession of land, which becomes instead the property of the state. The main policy however, has been to encourage settlement as a way of confining nomadic tribes within state boundaries and weakening tribal organisation and loyalties.

A problem of encouraging nomads to settle is to make agriculture successful in an environment that is short of water. In Saudi Arabia it has been estimated that even with the fullest application of irrigation, at least 80% of the country would remain as desert. Pastoral nomadism represents a remarkable adaptation to this marginal kind of environment, so that if all nomads were settled vast but seasonally restricted pastures would remain unutilised.

Traditional Bedouin existence has been described as the symbiosis of man and camel. It is the camel that enables the Bedouin to exploit the desert. It provides him with shelter, food, warmth and transport. Camel hair is woven into tents, camel dung is used as fuel and camels' milk provides nourishment, either fresh, since camels lactate at least eleven months a year, or preserved as cheese or clarified butter. Not only is the camel used for riding and carrying but it can go for much longer periods than man without water, and is able to drink otherwise unpalatable brackish water, turning it into nourishing liquid for man. So the Bedouin is able to move over the desert taking advantage of seasonal and geographical variations in occurrence of pastures.

Camels have made up the majority of tribal herds; sheep and goats are herded too but these, needing more frequent food and water, have to be kept nearer the fertile areas on the fringes of the desert. But, as camels are losing commercial value, being replaced by the Landrover and tractor, many more Bedouin have turned to herding sheep and goats to be sold in the towns as a means of entering into the modern market economy. In this way they can rise above a subsistence economy and make a significant contribution to the food supply. In Saudi Arabia and Syria a large proportion of goats, sheep and camels are under the care of the Bedouin and provide an important source of animal protein. An immediate result of this has been a tendency to over-graze, but it has been suggested that if the livestock industry were developed it could provide future occupation for the Bedouin.

Sedentarization is an inevitable part of the general social change taking place in the Middle East today, resulting in a spectrum of different lifestyles among the Bedouin. There are the completely nomadic, still living the traditional desert existence, and the semi-nomadic, herding and cultivating or being employed in industry or agriculture part of the year. Others have been drawn completely into urban life. In Saudi

Arabia many Bedouin were attracted into the developing oil industry in the fifties, to work as unskilled labourers, and remained there. Others become sedentary for all practical purposes but return to the desert each summer.

Julia Stephens

SELECT BIBLIOGRAPHY
Abou-Zeid, A.M., *Nomadism and Sedentarisation in the Arab World: A Select Annotated Bibliography,* Bulletin of the Institute of Arab Research and Studies, No. 3, March, 1972
Awad, M., *Settlement of Nomadic and Semi-Nomadic Tribal Groups in the Middle East,* ILO Review 79, No. 1, 1959
Clarke, J.I., Fisher, W.B., *Populations of the Middle East and North Africa,* University of London, 1972
Leiden, C. (ed.) *The Conflict of Traditionalism and Modernism in the Muslim Middle East,* Austin, Texas, 1969

9   The Berbers of North Africa

The Berbers are the original indigenous inhabitants of the North African littoral, concentrated in the fertile areas of the coastal plains and the mountains behind, and isolated from the rest of Africa by the Sahara desert. They originate from the Caspian culture of prehistoric North Africa but no longer present a common ethnic origin, having been subjected to continuous migrations and invasions from the Mediterranean, Asia Minor and sub-Sahel Africa. The Berber tribes were eclectic, willingly accepting parts of the civilisations of their invaders and often adapting them to their own purposes, but always maintaining their own identity. It was only with the Arab invasions after AD 642 that a more permanent influence came into North Africa.

The initial Arab invasions, numerically very small, met with considerable resistance from the Berbers because of the Arab policy of excluding the indigenous population from the benefits of conversion — benefits of tax exemption and administrative power. Despite the invasions of the 11th century — said to have involved the migration of between 300,000 and one million Arab nomads over a period of 50 years — the essential character of North Africa remained Berber.

The divisions that arose were not based on ethnic or religious differences. The Berbers willingly accepted Islam, even though they often only grafted it on to their own animism. They even founded dynastic empires — the Fatimids, the Zirids, the Almoravids, the Almohades, to name but the most important — and extended Islam northwards into Spain and southwards into the Sudan. It was rather the cultural, and sociological distinctions between urban commerce and rural tribalism, which developed to distinguish the Berbers today.

The great North African cities, because of their dependence on commerce, were open to the normative influences of Sunni Islam and formed part of the wider Muslim world of the Middle East and Asia. The distinctive features of Berber society, essentially rural and sedentary, gradually disappeared and were replaced by the cosmopolitan values of Muslim civilisation. Arabic, as a religious language and as the lingua franca of the western Muslim world, gradually replaced Berber. Muslim law and the Malakite rite were used instead of tribal customary law, and Berber oral literary traditions were subordinated to the Arabic literature of Andalous and Ifriquia. The tribal Berbers responded initially by espousing extreme and/or heretical forms of Islam — Kharijism, Shi'ism and the Ibadi rite — some of which have lasted into this century, notably in the Algerian Mzab and the Island of Djerba in Tunisia. Later on, as the predatory centralised power of the city-based sultanates or the Turkish Deys and Beys increased, the Berbers were forced back into the mountainous areas where geography gave them a precarious autonomy. Yet this did not imply cultural or economic isolation, only a refusal to recognise central authority or to pay taxes where central authority was too weak to assert its power.

Berber minority status, if it exists at all, is a result of North Africa's colonial experience, for when the French occupied North Africa (Algeria in 1839, Tunisia in 1881 and Morocco in 1912) they rapidly identified cultural, sociological and linguistic differences between plains and townspeople on the one hand and mountain peoples on the other. The former they claimed were Arab — because they usually spoke Arabic — and the latter were

Berber. In addition, since the mountain peoples were much more difficult to suppress and because their version of Islam appeared rather heterodox, the French assumed that they were ethnically different, but more easily assimilable to European culture. France therefore subjected Berber regions to different regimes of administration from the 'Arab' regions, tried to foster Berber culture and language — particularly in Morocco — and used the Berber reserves as a recruiting ground for the French army. The major Berber areas were the Grand and Petit Kabylie, the Aures and the Hodna in Algeria and the Rif, Middle Atlas, High Atlas and the Anti-Atlas in Morocco. Berber-speakers in these areas ranged from 60 to 100% of the population, with three main dialects, which were not mutually intelligible.

The Berbers reacted to this policy in two ways. Firstly the process of Arabisation progressed at a very rapid rate. In areas in which previously only Berber had been spoken, Arabic became an essential second language, and, in some cases, the sole language. Berber customary law, explicitly preserved within the French-administered legal system, was increasingly and often voluntarily superseded by Muslim religious law and Berbers often became conscious of their membership of a wider national grouping. On the other hand, Berbers took advantage of their new economic and commercial opportunities; to some extent this was in response to the over-population and poor resource base in Berber areas. The *Rifis,* from 1870 on, migrated annually to the Oranais where they worked for French colon farmers. After 1870 the *Kabyles* began to move into the Algiers area, particularly Algiers itself after 1900, and formed a new urban lumpen proletariat. The same thing happened after 1920 in Casablanca with migrants from all over Morocco; and all Berber groups supplied recruits to the French army.

During the struggles for independence, Berbers took a leading part in the fighting. The Algerian Revolution began in the Kabyle and the Moroccan Army of Liberation started in the Rif in 1953/54. As a result Berbers were strongly represented in the armies of the new national states and in their new police forces. Their presence in government was far less and one of the major problems which first faced the governments of independent Algeria and Morocco was how to integrate the Berbers — in view of their previous special treatment by the French — into a unitary state.

Very often Berbers felt shut out and isolated from central government. On occasion their patrons in central administration under the French lost their influence under the new regimes and tribal groups suffered accordingly. This was reflected in Morocco during the first three years of independence, by two major tribal uprisings and constant rural agitation against Istiqlal, the urban nationalist group which had led the independence struggle. Uprisings occurred in Morocco in the Rif, at Taza and in the Middle Atlas, yet although these were crushed by the new army those involved were not necessarily severely punished. Indeed, the monarchy used the uprisings as an excuse to destroy the political power of Istiqlal. The Berbers made their feelings of exclusion from central power explicit and this resentment was formalised — with encouragement by the monarchy — in the formation of an explicitly Berber-based political party in 1958.

In Algeria, Berber resentment was much slower to appear and when it did, did not show such violent features. In fact, it was largely a reaction to the Algerian government's consistent policy of Arabisation. This manifested itself by the exclusion of Berbers from government and by the extension of land reform and social reform into those areas where social structures had been least affected by French colonisation — *la Berberie*. In Tunisia however, the isolated pockets of Berbers have not been subjected to any problems by independence, largely because of their very small numbers.

Indeed, it is only in Morocco that a Berber minority problem really exists and even here the problem is faced less by Berbers as a distinct ethnic minority than by smaller tribal groups attached to particular patrons who occupy key positions in central government. The most recent published attempt against King Hassan — the 'events' of 3 March 1973 — involved a tribal revolt near to Gwilmima in the Atlas. Undoubtedly this revolt was bloodily crushed and it is certain that those involved were Berbers. Yet, although opposition groups abroad seem to have been involved, the real cause for the revolt was simply that the tribal factions were economically very deprived and felt that central government was ignoring their problems. In this respect they acted in an identical fashion to Arab-speaking peasants in the Gharb plains who revolted in 1970 against large landlords in their area.

Berber-speakers in Morocco are estimated to comprise 40% of

the population — about 6 million — but most of them, particularly the men, speak Arabic as well. The importance of Berber as a language is further reduced by constant migration to the towns, where Arabic is an essential means of communication and where typically Berber social structures are rapidly eroded by normative Arab structures.

The real minority groups in both Morocco and Algeria are the under-employed peasantry — Arab as well as Berber — and the unemployed lumpen proletariat in North African towns, many of whom are of Berber origins. It remains to be seen whether the economic policies of Algeria will eventually aid these groups and whether Morocco can develop the policies necessary to contain their growing discontent.

George Henderson

SELECT BIBLIOGRAPHY

Abdel Krim et la Republique du Rif, Maspero, 1976
Berque, J., *French North Africa,* Faber, 1967
Bidwell, R., *Morocco under Colonial Rule,* London, 1973
Chaliand & Minces, *L'Algerie Independante,* Maspero, 1972
Crapanzano, V., *The Hamadsha,* California, 1973
Evans-Pritchard, *The Sanusi of Cyrenaica,* Oxford, 1949
Gellner & Micaud, *Arabs and Berbers,* London, 1973
Gellner, E., *Saints of the Atlas,* London, 1967
Hoffman, G., *The Structure of Traditional Rural Moroccan Society,* The Hague, 1967
Maher, V., *Women and Property in Morocco,* Cambridge, 1974
Maxwell, G., *Lords of the Atlas,* London, 1966
Mercer, J., *Spanish Sahara,* London, 1975
Montagne, R., *The Berbers, Their Social and Political Organisation,* London, 1973
Palazzoli, C., *Le Maroc Politique,* Paris, 1975
Sweet, L.E., *Peoples and Cultures of the Middle East,* New York, 1970
Waterbury, J., *The Commander of the Faithful,* London, 1970
Waterbury, J., *North for the Trade,* California, 1972

10 The Bretons

An acute problem for France today is regionalisation, and Brittany exemplifies this: remote, inhospitable and bereft of natural resources, it possesses a cultural identity distinct from that of 'mainstream' France (of which it became part in 1789), and which it believes exploits and neglects it. Brittany's own problem is three-fold: economically it is underdeveloped, has suffered from lack of infrastructure and from high emigration; politically, it has yet to achieve the ideal mix of State and local control; psychologically, it seeks to preserve and to express an identity.

Under the State's continuing policy of deconcentration four of Brittany's five departments were in 1956 declared one of France's 22 'régions de programme', for purposes of economic planning. In 1964 a 'préfet de region' was appointed with his own regional mission and the *Commission de Developpement Economique Régional* was formed, an advisory body but nonetheless significant. From 1974 the Commission was replaced by a regional assembly with increased powers, including its own financial resources. The assembly is a representative body, elected indirectly, deciding the use of its own budget, and is consulted on the use of the State budget and on its economic plan. Final power however still remains with the State's representative, the regional prefect, in order to safeguard 'la France une et indivisible', a key Gaullist slogan. The French opposition parties and many Bretons advocate decentralisation rather than deconcentration, in order to achieve a kind of federalism. The Union of the Left would make Brittany a 'collectivité territoriale', with a directly elected assembly with its own executive and financial powers and with the prefect replaced by a Government commissioner, a link between region and State.

A similar plan of regional reform is favoured by CELIB, the *Comité d'Etude et de Liaison des Interêts Bretons,* which would also reform local government within the region by replacing the four departments with ten to twenty *pays*, in size midway between *commune* and *department*. But both CELIB and the national opposition parties are regarded by many Bretons as too slow and ineffective: hence the support for more radical groups such as *Strollard ar Vro* (the Breton party) the *Union Democratique Bretonne*, the *Parti Communiste Breton*, or the terrorist *Front de Liberation de la Bretagne*. While all these groups are united in their wish to see Brittany achieve independence within a French federal system, they split over their conception of the new society they wish to see. The broadest split is ideological, between *Strollard ar Vro* (SAV), which wishes to build a society based on class cooperation, and the left-wing groups to which such a concept is unacceptable. Additionally, SAV and the Left seek to win change through political means while the FLB concentrates on military action: it groups seven different wings, of which only two are well known. The FLB–LNS *(pour la Liberation Nationale et le Socialisme)* is socialist and revolutionary, while the FLB–ARB *(Armée Republicainé Bretonne)* is reckoned more nationalistic. Its exploits have included a number of spectacular bombings such as the destruction of a television transmitter at Roc'h Tredudon in 1974.

All political opposition to the State policy of deconcentration has to face the central dilemma of deciding whether to settle for limited reform by working within the established system or to build the revolution. So far it is reformist groups like CELIB which have done most for Brittany.

Economically deconcentration has paid some dividends. Brittany's population was in steady decline until 1954, but the influx of industry since then has reversed this, with emigration dropping steeply. There has nevertheless been a massive rural exodus and a major shift from agriculture into industry and services. Infrastructure has been improved, but there are still too many young people migrating (within Brittany to Rennes, and to other parts of France) and there are too few jobs, especially skilled ones. Depression continues: in 1971 Breton wages averaged 17% lower than the rest of France. Brittany is developing more slowly than the rest of the country.

By tradition conservative, Brittany is giving increasing support to the Left, which gained 27.9% of the vote in 1958 but 37.2% in

1973. There is no prospect at present that Brittany will grow richer by comparison with those parts of France nearer the centre of the EEC, and its relative poverty seems likely to continue, marked by emigration, low wages, poor working conditions and a lack of social facilities. Increased political polarisation is possible, and a victory of the Union of the Left perhaps offers hope of a starting point for the solution of Brittany's problems, by transferring the search for remedies to a regional base.

As to the Breton minority parties themselves, they will continue to have an important role as a channel of information to the world about the position of Brittany as a colony. They have tried to radicalise the policies of the Left by giving Mitterand their conditional support. Probably the UDB has the brightest prospects, as it is both better organised and more representative than the other Breton parties.

The essential problem the Breton parties face is to discover how to give back to the Bretons their dignity, something for which the Government's limited granting of economic advantages is no substitute. As Michel Philipponneau wrote in his *Debout Bretagne*, 'the greatest crime committed by the Gaullists in Brittany is to have attacked the dignity of the Bretons, is to have tried to transform a noble, proud people, who are generous but thirsty for justice, into a people submissive, prostrate, and who are searching for charity from the more skilful people, which is given as long as they stay silent'.

C.S.B.

SELECT BIBLIOGRAPHY

Caerleon, R., *La Révolution Bretonne Permanente,* La Table Ronde, 1969
Flatres, P., *La Région de l'ouest,* PUF, Paris, 1964
Guichard, O., *Aménager la France,* Laffont-Gonthier, 1965
Lebesque, M., *Comment Etre Breton: Essai sur la Democratie Francaise,* Editions du Seuil, Paris, 1972
Lerhun, P-Y., *Géographie Economique de la Bretagne,* Editions Breiz, 1972
Mayo, P.E., *The Roots of Identity,* Allen Lane, London, 1975
Philipponeau, M., *Debout Bretagne,* Presse Universitaires Bretonnes, St Brieuc, 1970

Pleven, R., *Avenir de la Bretagne,* Clamann-Levy, Paris, 1961
Serant, P., *La France des Minorités* Lafont, Paris, 1965

11   Burma: Separatism as a Way of Life

Burma achieved independence on 4 January 1948 there have
been resistance forces fighting the government and demanding
autonomy for groups who regard themselves as separate and
nationally distinct for every moment of the subsequent
twenty-seven years. Yet only for about two weeks in February
1949 did it ever appear probable that separatism could overthrow
the government and achieve its end. Today there are three major
separatist challenges to the central government: those of the
Shans, the Kachins, and the Karens. Under present day
circumstances none of them seems to have the slightest prospect
of succeeding. Yet each of them seems determined to fight on,
without regard to the end.

   The origin of this impasse is to be found in the peculiar
demographic structure of Burma. Between two-thirds and
three-quarters of the population regard themselves as one
people, with a living culture and a strong national tradition: these
are the Burmese. The remainder have no sense of identity
whatever with the Burmese. To them, assimilation would mean
subjection. Their strength is in their separateness. And yet
Burma is their homeland also. Only one group, the Shans, have a
really important 'base' outside Burma. The remaining minorities
spill over into neighbouring countries, but their motherland is
Burma. Of the total population of 27,500,000, there are
19,000,000 Burmese (including 2,000,000 Arakanese and
750,000 Mons), 2,800,000 Karen, 2,075,000 Shan, 750,000 Chin,
500,000 Kachin, 200,000 Palaung, 90,000 Naga, 60,000 Akha,
50,000 Lahu, 40,000 Lisaw, 30,000 Kadu, 30,000 Wa.

   The *Burmese* inhabit the great central plain, which they have
occupied since about AD 800. They are Theravada Buddhists,
with a strong sense of history and a strong sense of national
identity, based upon a popular folk literature and a common

life-style without important differences between rich and poor. The *Arakanese* are a separate branch of the Burmese, whose language varies a little more than Yorkshire does from standard English. They have been more exposed to Indian culture, and they include some Muslims. Their province was the first to come under British rule (1826) and the Arakanese elite has progressed furthest in higher education. The *Mons* or Talaings may perhaps be compared to the ancient Britons, though their culture was overlaid by the Burmese only in the 19th century.

The *Shans* are a branch of the great Tai people, numbering altogether perhaps 85–90 millions, and settled in China, Laos, Thailand, Assam, Vietnam, as well as Burma. The Shans have a written literature, mainly employing the Tai script though some use Burmese. They are Theravada Buddhists; they practise wet-rice cultivation like the Burmese, and they inhabit the upland valleys. They regard themselves as a race of rulers.

The *Kachins* also have a fierce, warlike tradition and have competed with the Shans for dominance in the northern highland country. The Kachins are also settled in Assam and in China. Unlike the Burmese and the Shans, they do not possess a common Kachin language. The main dialect is Jinghpaw (which also means 'a man'), and others are Maru, Rawang, Atsi and Lashi. Jinghpaw was first reduced to writing by an American missionary, and is now communicated through the Roman script. The Kachins were traditionally cultivators of upland dry-rice, but many are now settled in the northern lowlands and grow wet rice.

The *Karens,* although the largest minority numerically, have throughout most of their history had to accept a subservient relationship to the Burmese. Their three main languages are Sgaw, Pwo, and Bwe. Their original homeland was in the hill running down between Burma and Thailand, but the pressure of Burmese raiding drove many Sgaw Karens to take refuge in the Irrawaddy delta, when this was an isolated swampland. Originally, the Karens were Animists (as many still are today) but some assimilated forms of Buddhism. They have no original written literature, but pioneer American missionaries transcribed Sgaw, and later the other tongues, into the Burmese script. Originally dry-rice cultivators, the majority today farm irrigated paddies.

The *Chins* are a hill people, similar to the Karens, though inhabiting the hills straddling the border with India, and on the other (Indian) side of the hills they are known as *Kuki*. Linguistically they are much more divided, and economically they are more backward, than the Karens and Kachins. The *Nagas* are kin to the more numerous Naga tribes on the Indian side of the border, but the Burma Nagas are more backward, and still inclined to head-hunting. The *Palaung* are a group suspended between the shifting hill cultivation of the hill tribes and the more settled ways of the Shans. They are important cultivators of tea. The *Wa*, often called the Wild Wa, are believed by themselves and others to be the original inhabitants of the hills. They have repulsed efforts to subjugate them through the ages. Throughout the centuries, the hill people rendered tribute to the valley and plainsdwellers, who deployed superior force, and have the advantage of straddling trade routes and dominating important crossing places on rivers. Only the Kachins challenged the plainsdwellers and set up their own system of tolls on trade routes into China.

The history of Burma has focussed upon the Irrawaddy. Power has always rested with the authority which dominated the central span and thereby dominated trade and also the main rice crop. At different periods, the Shans and the Mons emerged as the dominant power, but by the end of the 18th century the struggle had been resolved in favour of the Konbaung dynasty of Burmese kings, ruling from their capital at Ava on the upper Irrawaddy. Their power was strong enough to strike terror into the hill tribes. The Chins tattooed the faces of their women to make them unattractive to the raiding Burmese. The Padaung (a branch of the Karens) gave their women giraffe necks, by throttling them with brass bangles, for the same purpose. The hill people trembled; but the Shans did not forget that they had once ruled Burma.

The Shans had about twenty separate states and about fifteen smaller fiefs. The states were ruled by hereditary *saophas,* or *sawbwas* as the Burmese called them. Each *sawbwa* had a miniature court, modelled on the court of the Burmese king. Each had a throne: but none dared challenge Burmese suzerainty by actually ascending the throne, except the most remote and the most powerful — Kengtung Sawbwa. By paying tribute to Ava, Bangkok, and Peking alike, the Kengtung Sawbwa kept his options open. When the Siamese tried to invade Kengtung in 1854, they suffered a bloody repulse.

The uneasy balance of power, or balance of terror, began to break down under pressures both internal and external. One of the most important of the new pressures appeared insignificant in its beginnings. In 1813, Adoniram Judson, an American Congregationalist turned Baptist, arrived at Rangoon, having been refused entry into British India. His mission was directed to the Burmese, whose language he first reduced to dictionary form, but by what appeared to be chance his message was seized upon by the Karens. After the first Anglo-Burmese war (1824–26), the Burmese authorities adopted a harsh, repressive policy against Christianity. The American missionaries made their headquarters at Moulmein in what was now British territory but the main expansion of Christianity occurred among the Karens of Bassein, still under Burmese rule. During the 1830s many thousands became Baptist Christians. Conversion was directed entirely by Karen pastors, and the movement, growing in secret, had much of the character of a resistance movement. For the first time, the Karens acquired a sense of self-confidence and social discipline.

Then, in the 1870s Karen and American missionaries moved north to Bhamo to work among the Kachins. Later, they established missions among the Chins, the Lahus, the Nagas, and other tribes. A clear pattern emerged. The Baptist Church appeared as the vehicle whereby the frontier tribes acquired organization, education, and the means to confront the Burmese overlord. The Americans and the Karens pioneered the work, but they rapidly sought out tribal leaders to take over leadership roles, remaining as teachers and advisers. The Baptists opened up the schools and provided the textbooks. As young Kachins, Chins, and others gradually worked their way towards higher education, they headed towards the Baptist bible college at Insein or the American Baptist Mission (ABM) college in Rangoon, where they could study for a Calcutta degree.

When, in 1920, a University of Rangoon was founded, the ABM was powerful engough to ensure that the new institution was divided into two colleges, University College, the government institution, where the students were Indians and Burmese, and Judson College, where they were Karens, with a few other tribal people.

The American missionaries had brought the frontier tribes into the 20th century without bringing them into 20th century

Burma. In line with Indian practice, the British distinguished between the plains districts, which were brought under a regular system of administration and a regular code of law, and the frontier areas which were left to get on with their own affairs, so long as they did not seriously disturb the peace. Not until 1925–7 did British columns penetrate the northern Kachin hills, and then only because the League of Nations was becoming restless about the continuation of slavery in the hills. When Burma was introduced to representative government and popular politics in the 1920s and '30s, the Shan States and the borderland became Excluded Areas, still handled exclusively by the British Governor and his officials and no concern of the Burmese politicians. The Karens of the plains did participate in the elections and the legislatures, but, they had their own separate constituencies.

The forces which were institutionalizing separatism received a mighty impetus in the second world war. Most of the Burmese political elite gave a warm welcome to the Japanese with their Co-Prosperity Sphere. A Burma National Army was formed to fight alongside the Japanese. The Shans gave a somewhat more tepid greeting but accepted the inevitable. Kengtung state was transferred to Thailand as a reward to Field Marshal Phibunsongkram. The Japanese advance stopped just short of the Kachin hills, which remained outside their control. British officers returned and recruited irregular levies for guerrilla warfare. The Japanese retaliated, and Kachin resistance grew. Although many of the levy officers were British (and also American), young Christian Kachins became leaders of missions. First the Chindits and then other allied forces moved into Kachinland. Briefly, these remote hills became part of the wider world.

Even more important was the Karen resistance. At first, the Karens were virtually on their own, but gradually they were supplied and reinforced from the air. They did much damage, and they suffered savage reprisals from the Japanese and also from the Burma National Army, but they still persisted. In the last phase, when the Japanese forces fell back, the Karens launched major attacks and virtually wiped out a Japanese army division.

The British announced that Burma's post-war political development would be put into cold storage for three years. But the dynamic former leader of the Burma National Army, Bogyok

Aung San, planned otherwise. He pressed the British government until in January 1947 Mr Attlee agreed to accept independence for Burma within twelve months. Aung San confronted every kind of problem; and he fully understood that history, ancient and recent, had fixed a gulf between the Burmese and the peoples of the hills. He met the frontier leaders in February 1947 at Panglong in the northern Shan States and within a few days succeeded in obtaining their agreement to participate in an independent Burma.

The Shan Sawbwas obtained assurances regarding the continuance of their traditional ruling powers. They were promised their own Shan State, and most important they were assured that if, after ten years, they no longer wished to belong to the Union of Burma they might secede and form a separate, independent state. The Kachins were also promised their own state, comprising the whole of Bhamo and Myitkyina Districts (in which they formed about half the population; the Shans were 45% of the population of the Shan State). The Chins were offered a separate, autonomous administration, the Chin Special Division. But Aung San utterly failed to win over the leaders of the Karens, who could not easily forget the sufferings of their people at the hands of the Burma National Army.

A new constitution was adopted by a Constituent Assembly in September 1947, on the eve of independence. The promises made in the Panglong agreement were honoured, though by now Aung San was dead. In addition, the constitution laid down that the small 'Red' Karen states (ruled by Sawbwas who were Karens), the Salween District, and other areas to be determined by a special commission, should all be formed into a Karen State, with the same status as the Shan State. Chapter X of the constitution was headed 'Right of Secession', and laid down a procedure for holding a plebiscite if demanded by two-thirds of one of the State Councils (each State had its own Council, composed of the MPs for the state, sitting in the Union Parliament). The constitution also provided machinery for 'admitting' a new state into the Union. A demand was immediately voiced for a separate Muslim state to be formed in that part of Arakan adjacent to East Pakistan. This was rejected, and by independence day a band of insurgents calling themselves *Mujahids* (Islamic freedom fighters) were under arms. This was a minor revolt: the major challenges to the elected government came from ideological rebels —

various types of Communists. Under pressure, the government relied heavily upon battalions raised on a 'tribal' basis from the minorities: the Chin Rifles, Kachin Rifles, and especially the Karen Rifles. The supreme commander of the armed forces was a Karen, as was the senior Brigade commander.

The Karen leaders were still demanding an autonomous state, and many were calling for complete independence. The countryside was overrrun by guerrilla bands, and the Karens formed, and armed, a Karen National Defence Organization (KNDO). Mutual suspicion between Burmese and Karens deepened. There were attacks on Karen villages, some timed for Christmas Eve, 1948, when most Karens were at church services and were vulnerable. Finally, there was a total breakdown. The KNDO attacked government positions joined by some (though by no means all) of the Kachin troops. The government was able to survive, and gradually began to move over to the offensive. The KNDO was pushed back, and the Kachin guerrillas, under their leader 'Brigadier' Naw Seng, retreated into the borderland with China. The threat to control Burma was over by the end of 1951: but the resistance continued unbroken. The government dealt with the situation by the classic device of 'Divide et Impera'. The Karens were denied the 'big' Karen state promised in the constitution. The Red Karens, the Karen-ni, were hived off in a separate state, Kayah, and some attempt was made to demonstrate that the Kayah was a different ethnic group from the Karen. The Karen State was enlarged, but its heartland remained in dispute between the KNDO and the Burma Army, which imposed a regime of military government. The Shan Sawbwas were suspected of aiding the KNDO, and their powers were gradually restricted. In April 1959 they signed an instrument whereby they surrendered all their powers (including the right to nominate the 25 Shan representatives in parliament), pressured into this surrender under the threat of losing their palaces and revenues.

The Kachins remained the 'loyal' minority. They voluntarily surrendered their constitutional right of secession. When the Karen Rifles were officially disbanded in 1949 (in reality they were all with the KNDO), the Kachin Rifles were expanded to six battalions. In 1960, however, they were required to accept a humiliating transfer of part of their territory to China. Long-drawn-out negotiations between Burma and China over the disputed frontier were brought to an end in 1960, and in general China dealt generously with 'Younger Brother'. China's prestige, however, required some concession from Burma in return for the renunciation of vast tracts previously shown on Chinese maps as part of China. Sixty square miles of Kachinland, around the Hpimaw Pass, had to be handed over. The Kachins resisted vigorously, but the price had to be paid.

By the general election of 1960, the government led by U Nu, which had directed affairs since 1947, was struggling for survival. Under pressure from the left, and the object of suspicion by the army and its commander, General Ne Win, pledges designed to appeal to different sections of the electorate were made. To obtain support from the minorities, he promised to establish new states for the Arakanese and the Mons; to get the support of the *sangha,* the monastic order (and also the important female vote), he promised to make Buddhism the official state religion. He won the election by a handsome majority. Buddhism was institutionalized as the state religion in 1961. After the cession of the Hpimaw area, this badly upset the Kachins: perhaps 40% or more of the Kachins are Christians, and the remainder are Animists. Nu's move looked like cultural imperialism (and it was implemented by the despatch of Buddhist missionaries into the frontier hills). A revolt began among the Kachins, leading to the formation of a Kachin Independence Army (KIA).

In this situation, General Ne Win seized power. A major reason that was given out was that the Union was on the point of breaking up. U Nu and his Cabinet were arrested, and beside the many Burmese sent to jail, a high proportion of frontier leaders were incarcerated, including the Kachin leader, the Sima Duwa, Sinwa Nawng, the president-elect. A former president, the Shan sawbwa, Sao Shwe Thaik, was killed resisting arrest. Ne Win attempted to deal with the minorities by a mixture of stick and carrot. By now, all the minority peoples — Karens, Shans, Kachins and Chins — had substantial guerrilla movements, fighting the Burma Army and maintaining a somewhat precarious hold over about 40% of Union territory. Ne Win re-equipped the army and air force and mounted powerful punitive expeditions. He also negotiated with the underground rebels. The only group to agree to terms were the KNDO, and in 1964 their leaders agreed (in the euphemistic language chosen for surrender) to 'enter the light'. The emergence of the KNDO bands, handing in their arms, was much publicized. They were 'resettled' (which involved a period in camps under army control) and most remained under strict police surveillance. The concession in return for the KNDO cease-fire was supposed to be a restoration of the 'big' Karen state, to be called *Kawthulay* ('golden flowery land'). This, however, was slow to eventuate, and soon the KNDO revolt was on again.

Ne Win intensified his 'stick' policy. All political parties were suppressed, except for his own Burma Socialist Programme Party *(Lanzin)*. All non-public institutions were nationalized in 1965: this included the hospitals and high schools founded by missionaries. For many years applications for entry by foreign missionaries had been refused, and those going on furlough were not permitted to come back. Finally, in 1966, all remaining missionaries were ordered out, except for a handful of Roman Catholics. The Christians were placed under close surveillance, and any activities on an inter-tribal basis (such as the Kachin Baptist mission to the Nagas) were suppressed. Ne Win still made occasional gestures towards the minorities, such as the setting up of an institute of national culture at Sagaing, in which the various arts and crafts of the Shans and the hill peoples were fostered.

After more than a decade, a new constitution was presented to the people for their consideration at a referendum in December 1973. The new constitution was ratified in January 1974. Burma now became the Socialist People's Republic of Burma with General Ne Win as president, supported by a number of institutions: the Council of Ministers, the Council of Attorneys (having the functions of the former Supreme and High Court), the Council of Inspectors, and a Council of State, being the standing representation of the people. Burma was grouped into a number of political rather than administrative divisions, run by popularly elected People's Councils meeting annually as the People's Congress. The new constitution swept away the whole apparatus of states for the minority peoples, de-emphasising their separate interests and reinforcing the common ideological cause. Nevertheless, the whole new structure had a narrowly Burmese flavour. Ne Win chose no important members of minorities for his ministers, and other high officials were Burmese.

Not surprisingly this political innovation gave fresh impetus to the separatist movements with more than two-thirds of the country under insurgency, and large areas beyong government control. The Shan state was overrun by rival guerilla forces: some represented former sabwas, some politically motivated — increasingly communist orientated; some fighting for the hill-tribes like the Wa; and some were war-lords on the old Chinese model. Stikes — the first since Ne Win's accession — and riots broke out in Rangoon, literally over the body of U Thant, former Secretary-General of the UN, and led to the imposition of Martial Law in December 1974. In May the following year, five Karen, Mons, Arakanese and Shan parties united to form the Federal National Democrativ Front in order to 'overthrow the one-party military dictatorship and establish a federal union of national self-determination'. The front hoped to seek the support of the Kachins and Chins, but were ambiguous about communist support. Increasingly these groups are involved in the growing of opium and the sale of heroin to support themselves — the government seized an opium refinery in Shan state during the fierce fighting in 1975 — and raising a levy on goods smuggled from Thailand through their territory for the Rangoon black market; perhaps other money comes from the ubiquitous CIA, who supported the Sawbwas.

Ne Win engaged in a considerable amount of diplomacy, with a visit to China presumably to obviate Chinese support for the KIA (although subsequently China continued its support to the Communist Party of Burma and whomsoever was fighting for it). Diplomatic relations were established with North Korea, Vietnam, and later Cambodia, and it was reported that Thailand was closing its consulate in Shan and had decided to repatriate all refugees from Burma, to put an end to operations against the Burmese government from within Thailand.

In 1976 the KNDU and the KIA joined forces with the Federal National Democratic Front, and there was a general agreement not to attack communist forces. Ne Win's Defence Minister resigned and soon afterwards a plot against Ne Win and the 'social and economic system' was discovered which he was thought to have condoned; many others were put on trial, but nevertheless Ne Win felt secure enough to lift Martial Law in September. (It had been estimated earlier that 25,000 rebels had been killed, 50,000 surrendered or captured, while the government forces had lost 10,000, largely in the fighting since the new Constitution).

Because the integrative factors remain weak, the 'balance of instability' is likely to continue: Ne Win's slogans and rallies have been seen to be no substitute for action, although ideological unity seemed a credible strategy. Caught in a historical trap, to allow separatist identity in Burma is to encourage competition: regionalism disintegrating into tribalism. Confrontation unites contradictory forces into stronger, if still geographically separate, opposition. But the only circumstances in which the Burma separatist movement might succeed would be if a powerful neighbour became committed to the movement. The Thais regard the Karen as a backward hill people, and while they are more likely to support their 'kith and kin', the Shans, separatism is not entirely dead in more stable Thailand and they would seem unwise to give it any impetus. China is firmly opposed to separatist movements, partly in mind of her own minority peoples, partly because, if her support for the Kachins led to the emergence of a Kachin state — independent of Burma but dependent on China — India would be provoked by this corridor to Nagaland, and to the strengthening of her own Naga separatists, by the Burma Nagas. There is really no solution in separatism: the Burmese, their hill cousins and others must learn to live together one day.

Hugh Tinker

SELECT BIBLIOGRAPHY

Kunstadter, P., ed., *Southeast Asian Tribes, Minorities and Nations,* Princeton, 1967
Tegenfeldt, H.G., *A Century of Growth: the Kachin Baptist Church of Burma,* Pasadena, 1974
Tinker, H., *The Union of Burma: A Study of the First Years of Independence,* London (4th Edit), 1967
Woodman, D., *The Making of Burma,* London, 1962

12   The Canary Islanders

The Canary archipelago has 1,171,000 inhabitants (1970), 3.5% of the population of Spain. The seven islands, 7300 sq.km. in area, lie from 100–400 km. off the coast of the Western Sahara. They were settled during the first centuries AD by Berbers from NW Africa; European exploration located the archipelago by about 1300. The French conquered three lesser islands in 1402–5 and at once sold these to the Spanish; a fourth, small island was absorbed by Spain in the next few decades; finally, between 1483–96, the Iberians subjugated the three largest islands.

The pre-conquest inhabitants of the archipelago may have numbered 50,000 people; many were killed during the conquest or sent to the Peninsula as slaves. The survivors mixed with the massive influxes of Spanish settlers and, between 1476–1525, of Berbers and Arabs caught on the adjacent coast by the Spaniards for slavery in the islands. The survivors of the island people found it expedient to forget their origins, and when in the early nineteenth century the first murmurs of independence were heard, one could say that the *guanches* and the descendants of the Spanish and other immigrants were already integrated to form a single group, the Canary Islanders. In 1860 this population stood at 237,000.

The archipelago's first independence claims, with their roots in an eighteenth century of disasters, were stimulated by the French Revolution and subsequently by the freedom struggles of Spain's American colonies. In 1852 discontent was calmed by the granting of 'free port' status to the islands, allowing economic development; at a further crisis-point in 1909, unrest was pacified by giving increased autonomy to the island councils, but only after troops had been sent to end the 'independence' of the town of La Laguna.

The current phase of discontent began when, from the time of the Civil War, Franco's policy for the Canaries was seen to be the suppression of the islands' special legislation and an increase in centralisation. The 1940–5 depression caused emigration to South America, especially to Venezuela. In the 1950's, as a century earlier, the spectacle of other peoples gaining independence — this time Africans — produced the non-violent 'Movement for Autonomy in the Canaries' (MAC), organised by intellectuals. During the strikes and demonstrations of 1961–62, the MAC drew support from the general discontent of the archipelago worker with conditions in Spain; there were two dozen MAC arrests.

In 1964 the MAC and other clandestine autonomy groups united as the 'Movement for the Self-determination and Independence of the Canary Archipelago' (MPAIAC); it was to be the militant arm of the 'Canary Workers Party' and of any other social classes wishing to join in the same aims. Dissenting smaller movements do exist at present, for example in favour of devolution rather than independence; MPAIAC often refers to the need for a 'United Canary Front'. The MPAIAC manifesto demands independence for reasons which can be divided into three groups. First, to allow access to those human rights denied equally to all Spanish citizens by the central government. Secondly, to permit the islanders to organise their administration, economy and culture according to the traditions and peculiar needs of the archipelago. Thirdly, to deal with the following wider economic and political aspects.

Government policy has favoured foreign investment and tourism and these now dominate the islands. The land, building, hotel and other tourist businesses are in the hands of Canadian, English, French, German, Swedish and U.S. organisations. The U.S. controls oil refining and distribution, the paper industries and one of the shipping companies. For the islander, the result has been that the cost of living and of property has risen far faster than have wages. 3% of the landowners control 75% of the irrigable land and, conversely 90% of the farmers occupy only 13% of the productive ground. Most of the big landowners are from the Peninsula or from abroad. Both France and the U.S. have military satellite bases on the islands and the airports have recently been modernised with U.S. aid in order to handle military planes. The U.S. and NATO use the Canaries as a platform for watching Africa. Spain allows the Portuguese and South African governments to use the islands.

The MPAIAC proposes the creation of a democratic socialist 'Guanche Republic', independent and part of Africa. Each island would have limited autonomy, with the pre-conquest form of administration and titles; major industries would be nationalised. Foreign investment would be limited to a maximum of 45% in any one enterprise, with one-third of the profits to be re-invested in the Canaries. Worker participation would be a minimum 15%; Unions would be established. Individual land-holding would be restricted to 5 hectares of irrigable and 10 hectares of non-irrigable land; foreigners would be limited to 2½ hectares. Excess and unused land would be redistributed and agricultural co-operatives encouraged.

The movement has been condemned both by the Madrid authorities and by the Republican government-in-exile. The MPAIAC has offered to negotiate but sees armed struggle as inevitable. In 1968 it was provisionally recognized by the Liberation Committee of the OAU which in 1975 was asked to provide military aid. There has been discussion of an equal-terms federation with an independent Western Sahara, somewhat comparable to that of the Cape Verde Islands with Guinea-Bissau.

As an independent state the Canaries would be far from the smallest at the U.N. According to the MPAIAC, the archipelago is sufficiently advanced economically and politically to survive. Yet whilst there is no doubt that the grievances listed in the movement's manifesto are widely held throughout the islands, the small scale of MPAIAC activities suggests that the people are not generally in favour of independence, however much they might welcome a large measure of devolution.

John Mercer

SELECT BIBLIOGRAPHY

Africa, 24 August 1973
Gibson, R., *African Liberation Movements,* Oxford University Press, London, 1972
Margarido, A., *'Les Iles Canaries entre l'Europe et l'Afrique',* Keesings, 9 September 1974
Mercer, J., *Canary Islands: Fuerteventura,* David & Charles, 1973
Moudjahid, El, Algiers, 21 July 1968

MPAIAC: *Nos Principes,* Algiers, 1967
      Memorandum Demande, Algiers, 1970
      The Canary Islands, Algiers, 1972
Revue Francaise: *D'etudes politiques Africaines,* 1968

13 The Catalans

Catalonia has always been the economic power-house of Spain with a reputation for efficient trading and profitable commercial interests. Even now there is something of a rivalry between Madrid and Barcelona to achieve recognition as the most important town in Spain. The Greeks, the Romans, and more particularly, the Phoenicians, brought the essence of a commercial culture with them when they arrived in this part of the Iberian peninsula. Seafaring and booming trade developed certain attitudes, and the Catalans soon had the reputation of being industrious, individualistic, assertive, uncompromising and haughty. The economic viability which had been created in the early days meant that the Catalans were always interested in their own self-determination and thus their struggles with the Castilians have always been more politically than culturally based.

 French influence too has consistently been strong. In 785 Charlemagne made an unsuccessful attempt to gain sovereignty, followed in 801 by Louis le Debonnaire's conquest of Barcelona. After eight years of misrule, the Earl deputed to supervise the area rebelled, and the Catalan separatist movement began. Years of toil and consolidation followed until, in the eleventh century, a comprehensive codification of laws began. The duties and rights of the Counts of Barcelona were clarified and all were obliged to participate in defence, civil matters (like the protection of strangers), and penal law. In the twelfth century came the union of Aragon followed quickly by that with Valencia, and in 1479 the tenuous unity of Spain came about with the help of alliances and marriages. Catalonia often looked to France for military and political support during the seventeenth century. Throughout this period Catalan institutions were being created and re-inforced: the Council of the Hundred, the General Deputation, various tribunals, administrative bodies, and a separate coinage. During this time also the Catalan language was in widespread use. More akin to medieval Provencal (the 'lang d'Oc') than Castilian, Catalan was the co-official language of Spain for a long time. It was a language of culture in the Middle Ages but Catalan literature is strictly medieval and the language never really adapted itself to the spirit of the Renaissance. It was the language of the royal court until the fifteenth century, of administration until the 1716 annexation to Castile, of education until the decree of 1768 (forbidding its use in schools), and of private deeds, wills and testaments until 1862 when Castilian was substituted. It had certainly ceased to be of major cultural importance before Catalonia lost its national independence in 1714, after the wars of the Spanish succession; but the importance of Catalan in legal, financial, and political terms was deliberately eroded by the Castilian government, for more political than cultural reasons.

At the beginning of the nineteenth century the Catalan national spirit was dormant and the Castilian government abolished Catalan penal law (1822), special tribunals (1834), coinage (1837) and regional administration (1845). After a period of sustained shock at the removal of the pillars of Catalan society, indignation set in. Rubio y Ors tried to revive the language and the Catalan press, poetry, and theatre started to show signs of life. Catalanism awoke to reality and its republican foundations were laid in 1886 with Almirall's 'Lo Catalanisme'. This left wing Catalanism which represented progress, free thought, and democracy, was counterbalanced by the development of right wing Catalanism (under Torras Y Bages) which represented faith, order and tradition. Neither, however, saw Catalonia as a nation, and it was not until Prat de la Riba's ideas for a federation of Catalan speaking lands — Valencia, the Balearic islands, and Catalonia — that any kind of unity of approach appeared.

The relative economic sophistication of Catalonia became important again, as the only region of the peninsula to experience any kind of industrial revolution. There were tariff troubles with the rest of Spain and the first labour disputes and anarchist outbreaks in the 1890's. Catalan nationalism continued to rise under the leadership of Prat de la Riba but it suffered a bad setback in 1903, from a combined opposition of radicals, anti-clericals, and republicans who thought that these separate issues were more important than nationalism. The sense of nationhood and desire for self-determination grew again however, culminating in 1922 when Macia formed a strong Catalan party. In 1931 he proclaimed the Catalan republic and became its first President. The Statute of Autonomy which was voted overwhelmingly by the Catalans was drastically reduced by the Cortes Constituyentes, and when Franco came to power the Catalans were denied any concessions to cultural, political, legal or economic independence. All political parties were declared illegal, complete control of economic policy was taken by Castile, and measures were taken against Catalan writers.

The nature of the contemporary Catalan fight is different, and in recent years the protests have been both stronger and more fundamental. Current feeling is that the struggle for independence must of necessity be a struggle against capitalism. The Catalan communist party is now the strongest of many Catalan parties working in their separate ways towards the destruction of an illiberal central government and the right to more freedom of choice, discussion, organisation and decision-making power. Since Juan Carlos acceded to the Spanish throne the Catalans, among others, have been shown unprecedented toleration. Their view, though, is undoubtedly that these incremental promises of movement are hardly worth considering. They named the royal *indulto* (political amnesty) an *insulto* as an apt comment on its derisory nature, and they remain sceptical about further democratic developments. Catalans have recently been attempting to liaise more with Galicians but the nature of each unrest is still so different that the preliminary contact has not so far produced any signs of organisation. The campaign for socialist autonomy can be expected to continue and to grow.

Catherine Akester

SELECT BIBLIOGRAPHY

Alba, V., *Catalonia,* Hurst, London, 1975
Madariaga, S. de, *Spain — A Modern History,* Cape, London, 1958
Morrow, F., *Revolution and Counter-Revolution in Spain,*

Pathfinder Press, New York, 1974
Pla, J., *Cataluna,* Destino, Barcelona, 1961
Rossinyol, J., *Le Probleme National Catalan,* Mouton, Paris, 1974
Sencourt, R. *Spain's Ordeal,* Longmans, London, 1940
Vilar, P., *La Catalogne dans l'Espagne Moderne,* Sevpen, Paris, 1962

14   The Chinese-Americans

The Chinese were the first large non-slave, non-white group of
immigrants to come to the United States. When they first arrived
in California during the 1849 gold rush, California's newly
written constitution defined the state as a white one;
naturalisation could be conferred only on European white people
and suffrage only to white male citizens. In 1850 non-white
persons were also excluded from giving evidence in court. In the
urban labour shortage the Chinese were accepted to perform
basic services such as laundering and cooking, but when Chinese
miners attempted to join white miners in search of gold,
anti-Chinese hostility — sabotage, harassment, and lynching
broke out.

California's developers, however, saw that this was a source of
cheap labour, and, as well as using the harassed miners, started
importing Chinese under contract to build the notorious West
coast railways such as the Central Pacific. The work was
particularly arduous amid California's hard rock structure,
conditions in the camps were bad with high mortality and low pay,
and white workers were treated preferentially. Later employed in
industrial work, by 1870 the Chinese constituted 14% of the
work-force in San Francisco. But the white labour movement
became instrumental in the passage of anti-Chinese exclusion
laws in 1882, and an anti-Chinese political platform became
essential to politicians seeking labour votes.

Out of the need for self-preservation, the Chinese gathered to
live in urban 'Chinatowns', developing their own institutions,
clans and secret societies. Until recently the population of these
'Chinatowns' was predominantly male: at first due to the male

contract labour system, and later because of the 1924
Immigration Act which forbade the entry of Chinese women into
the U.S. for settlement. In 1945 this Act was repealed for the
wives of Chinese-Americans men who had served in the war; and
after the arrival of thousands of war-brides, and the post-war
baby-boom, the sex-ratio has become approximately equal for the
first time, though there remain many elderly bachelors. The 1970
census gave 339,243 Chinese-Americans, of whom the vast
majority live in urban areas. Merchant businessmen form the
Chinatown establishments, but most of those living there are first
generation Chinese-Americans and newly arrived immigrants
from Hong-Kong and Taiwan, low-income families and small
shopkeepers. About 40% fall below Federal poverty standards,
and unemployment is higher than the national average.
Chinese-American workers, especially in restaurants, laundries
and sub-contracting garment factories — 'sweat-shops' —
commonly do not receive the legal minimum wage and work long
hours in unsanitary and unsafe conditions. Housing is
substandard and crowded with a decline in the number of
low-rent units and the rise in the population. In San Francisco,
Chinatown had the highest tuberculosis and suicide rates in the
U.S. for 1972. There are few Chinese speaking doctors, dentists
and psychiatrists and limited public health services available.
Crime, which previously took the form of mainly self-contained
racketeering, has spread outwards to become a serious youth
gang problem.

Since the 1940s, more Chinese have achieved a higher level of
education, and although discrimination among the professions
and blue-collar occupations has prevented their taking their due
proportion of job opportunities (in California 29% of Chinese
males and 23% females had one or more years of college
education, but they formed only 17% of the professions), there
has been a move towards suburban living. As with many ethnic
groups in the U.S., this has raised the ambiguous problem of
identity among the Chinese-Americans. Language lessons for
children after school as well as cultural centres for adults have
been established. There has been a controversy over 'bussing'
away from community schools, and the content of state school
curricula which are seen to ignore not merely the depth and
strength of Chinese culture but the history of Chinese-
Americans. A Supreme Court decision of 1974 held that all

non-English speaking children have the right to access to non-English education, and many feel that not enough is being done to enforce it. Encouraged by minority rights movements among other racial groups, and perhaps by the rise of China as a great power, as well as by the resistance of Asians to American dominance in South East Asia, Chinese-Americans can feel less inferior to white America, and they see bilingual education as a solution to past shame and under-achievement, and becoming paradoxically more self-assuredly American.

L.B.F./P.S.

SELECT BIBLIOGRAPHY

Dinnerstein, L., Reimers, D.M., *Ethnic Americans — A History of Immigration and Assimilation,* Dodd, Mead, New York, 1975
Journal of Social Issues, 29, No. 2, 1973
Mann R., *Community Development and Attitudes Towards Chinese: The Mining Camp Experience,* Organisation of American Historians (Sixty-Seventh Meeting), Denver, April 1974
Melendy, B., *The Oriental Americans,* Twayne, New York, 1972
Tung, W.L., *The Chinese in America 1820-1973,* Oceana, Dobbs Ferry, New York, 1973
Weiss, M.S., *Valley City: A Chinese Community in America,* Cambridge, Mass., 1974

15   The Copts

According to ancient tradition, St. Mark the Evangelist was the founder of the Church of Egypt, otherwise known as the Coptic Church. When the Roman Empire was divided at the death of the Emperor Theodosius (AD 395), Egypt went with the eastern division, known as the Byzantine Empire. The separation of the Egyptian Church from the Christian community took place later at the Council of Chalcedon (AD 451). The faith is known as the Monophysite Faith which acknowledges that Christ was God and

Man, but affirms that both natures were united in Him, instead of being co-existent (which implies imperfect union).

The Empress Pulcheria disestablished the National Church of Egypt, and granted much of its property to the small minority of Egyptians who remained within the Christian community. These formed what was afterwards called the Melkite, or Imperial Church, as opposed to the National Church. Then, in 641, Egypt fell to the Arab Muslims. Resistance was ruthlessly suppressed, and after an uprising in 830 Christians were left for the first time a minority in the land. From the ninth century until the nineteenth the Copts were persecuted by their Muslim rulers, whether Arab, Circassian or Ottoman. Their Churches were destroyed, their services prohibited, their books burnt, their elders imprisoned and even murdered. After the French and English conquest of Egypt, Turks re-occupied the country. In the anarchy which followed, Mohammed Ali, a European of Christian ancestry and an able if unscrupulous ruler, employed an increasing number of Christians in government service, since they were found to be better educated than the Muslims.

When Egypt was occupied by the British in 1882, many government servants were Copts, who had been reduced to little more than 700,000 in a population of seven million. An attempt was then made to encourage Muslims to take 'their proper place in their own country', and Copts felt treated with disfavour and injustice by those to whom they had looked for help. However, in 1884 they were freed from all legal disabilities and today number nearly seven million themselves.

The current Egyptian Government limits freedom of worship by retaining a law issued in 1856 under the Ottoman Empire, under which a presidential decree is required to build or repair a church. (No permit is granted if the site is near a mosque, government agency, bridge, canal, square or the River Nile; or if a neighbour or the Muslim sheikhs object). The government has confiscated all hospitals built and administered by the different Christian denominations, together with church lands, some schools and other property, without compensation.

Islam, Egypt's state religion, and the Koran, the major source of Egyptian law, have been interpreted by the Grand Mufti as follows: (a) Muslims should never accept non-Muslims as full and equal partners in the nation. (b) A Christian who embraces Islam is not considered apostate, whilst a Muslim who becomes a

Christian is, and deserves to be put to death even if formerly a
Christian. According to Egyptian law no non-Muslim can inherit
from a Muslim even within the same family. Furthermore, the
Supreme Court has decided that the testimony of Christians
cannot be accepted because Christians are infidels, and infidels
may not testify against Muslims. The Egyptian mass media
continuously characterises Christians as infidels who deserve to
be isolated or converted. Christian scholars are denied the
freedom to publish books in response.

Copts, accounting for 20–25% of the population, are drafted in
proportionately higher numbers than Muslims into the armed
forces, but are deprived of senior positions. Of 55 ministers, only
two Copts are in the cabinet; there are only two Coptic
ambassadors out of more than 100, and one Coptic dean out of
160; no Copt is a police commissioner, provincial governor or city
manager. Military and police colleges restrict Christian admission
to as little as 5%; colleges of medicine do not accept Christians in
their departments of gynaecology or obstetrics. Al-Azhar
University does not accept any Christians in its non-religious
colleges and the government refuses to allow the establishment of
a Christian university.

There are approximately 100,000 Copts in Sudan, served by
twenty Churches and two bishops. There are Coptic communities
and churches in Israel, Jordan, Kuwait, and Lebanon, with a
bishop residing in Jerusalem. In addition, the Pope of Alexandria
is the supreme head of the Ethiopian Church. Recently Copts
have been emigrating further afield; there are 100,000 Copts in
North America, served by ten churches in Canada and the U.S.A.
50,000 Copts in Australia are served by five churches in Sydney
and Melbourne. There are Coptic communities and churches in
France and England.

Shawky F. Karas

SELECT BIBLIOGRAPHY

Bucher, H., *Middle East,* Pendulum Press, New Haven, 1973
Chanleur, S., *Histoire des Coptes d'Egypte,* La Colombe, Paris, 1960
Hussein, Mohammed (trans by Michael Clairman) *Class conflict in
Egypt 1945–71,* New York, 1973

Masriya, Y., *A Christian Minority: The Copts in Egypt* in *Case Studies on Human Rights and Fundamental Freedoms* Vol 4, Nijhoff, The Hague, 1976
Meinardius, O.F.A., *Christian-Egyptians: Faith and Life,* American University Press, Cairo, 1970
Wahir, E., *A Lonely Minority: the Modern Story of Egypt's Copts,* Morrow, New York, 1963

16   Cornish Nationalism

Cornwall forms a promontory of land in the South West of the British Isles, bounded by sea on three sides and joined to England by its Eastern border. For most of its length this border follows the course of the River Tamar, the traditional dividing line between Cornwall and the neighbouring English county of Devon. The present population is between 350 and 400,000 and becoming rapidly unbalanced due to the influx of retired people, and the departure of young people who cannot find employment.

The Cornish people are Celtic in origin, closely related to the Welsh and the Bretons and less closely to the Irish, Manx and Scots. After the demise of the Roman Empire in the 5th century AD, the Anglo-Saxon invasions of the British Isles resulted in the gradual retreat of the native Celts to an area stretching from Dumnonia (Devon and Cornwall) across Wales to Cumberland and Scotland. As their retreat continued, the Cornish, Welsh and Scots became isolated, and their culture and languages developed separately and distinctly. The conquest of Cornwall was not completed until the year 936 and for another 500–600 years it enjoyed a semi-independent status.

In 1497, under Henry VII, taxes were being raised to finance a war against Scotland; taxes which many Cornish people refused to pay and which led to a 15,000 strong Cornish army marching on London. These rebels were eventually defeated at the Battle of Blackheath on 17 June 1497. Soon afterwards, the Dissolution of the Monasteries and the Reformation in the 16th century signalled the beginning of the suppression of the Cornish language. In 1549 the imposition of the English Prayer Book led to another unsuccessful rebellion which was only subdued with very great force. The elimination of the Cornish language in religious worship undoubtedly accelerated its decline. Towards the end of the 18th century, the last monoglot speakers died but bilingual Cornish speakers survived for another hundred years. The early years of the 20th century at last saw the trend reversed with the formation of organisations to encourage the revival of the language and the rebirth of nationalist aspirations.

The main organisation seeking self government is Mebyon Kernow (Sons of Cornwall) formed in 1951, which now aims to contest all Cornish constituencies in the next General Election, after contesting local government elections since the mid sixties. In spite of the efforts by Mebyon Kernow and by the purely cultural organisation Kesva an Tavas Kernewek (The Cornish Language Board), the English orientated educational system still prevails. The majority of school teachers are not Cornish and little progress has been made in the teaching of the Cornish language and Cornish history in schools. Similarly, newspapers, radio and television do little to promote Cornish culture. In spite of this, there are more people capable of speaking Cornish today than at any time during the last 250 years, mainly due to the introduction of evening classes.

The main threat to Cornwall at the present time is that of incorporation into an English South West region. This has been happening gradually over recent years and the prospect of devolution for the English regions brings this possibility closer. The Cornish resent the amalgamation of Devon and Cornwall police authorities, local weather boards, and hospital administration. The establishment of South West Economic Planning Council and the subsequent inclusion of parts of Cornwall in economic planning areas which include large areas of Devon, is seen as a threat, as is the expansion of the City of Plymouth on the other side of the river Tamar.

Unemployment remains high owing to the fact that many industries in Cornwall are subsidiaries of English firms based in the Midlands or the South East. At times of economic crisis the distant 'satellite' factories are the first to close. Cornwall is over-dependant on tourism, by nature a seasonal industry, leaving high unemployment during the winter, while traditional activities such as agriculture and fishing do not receive the financial support they need. Employers in Cornwall, are considered actively anti-Cornish and cases are quoted where employees have been victimised for political activities in connection with Mebyon Kernow.

There can be little doubt, however, that Cornish national consciousness is greater today than it has been at any time in recent history owing to a determined reaction among Cornish people against the factors undermining their identity.

A.M. Casey

BIBLIOGRAPHY

Beresford-Ellis, P., *The Cornish Language and its Literature*, Routledge & Kegan Paul, 1974
Whetter, J., *A Celtic Tomorrow — Essays in Cornish Nationalism*, M.K. Publications, Padstow, 1973

17   The Corsicans

Regionalism is increasing rapidly in France as grievances grow against increased economic centralisation, but Corsican separatists and autonomists regard their cause as the most important. This island of 8722 square kilometres spent 600 years under Rome, 200 under Pisa, 500 ruled by Genoa, and 22 years of national independence under Pascal Paoli before being ceded to France in 1768 against the wishes of the Corsicans. Today, of 240,000 inhabitants, only 112,000 are indigenous; (as opposed to the entire population of 300,000 in 1900); 51,000 are Sardinians and Moroccans; 17,000 are French Algerians, 60,000 from the mainland. 400,000 Corsicans have emigrated in search of employment, and live abroad.

From initial protests in 1960 against the establishment of a nuclear base at Bologne, Corsican discontent has grown into a serious problem for the French government. There are 5 legally recognised groups — *Parti du Peuple Corse,* PPC; *Parti Corse Pour le Progres,* PCP; *Parti du Peuple Corse pour l'Autonomi,* PPCA; *Parti corse pour le Socialisme,* PCS; and the most important *l'Action Regionaliste Corse,* ARC; and as many clandestine organisations, who are mostly responsible for the growth of violence from 5 bomb explosions in 1970 to 150 in 1975.

This large *departement* has become entirely dependent on viticulture and tourism, both under the control of non-Corsicans. In the summer, 1 million tourists occupy the vast number of chain hotel beds (95 hotels in 1969, with 3040 beds; 365 in 1975 with 11,419), which have replaced traditional Corsican small hostelries, and by-pass local produce with imported provisions. (Australian lobsters are flown in, although the Corsican fishing industry includes them in their catch). A scheme to resettle Algerian *colons* on agricultural land with low mortgages not available to Corsicans, led to almost complete control of vineyards by non-Corsicans, as well as the reduction of other agricultural produce on that land. 5,600 Corsican peasants own 6,000 hectares, of which 5,000 are under viticulture, while 500 individuals own a further 29,000 hectares, of which 25,000 are under wine-production. Only 10% of the wine is of controllable quality, and this has led to national scandals, upon which the Corsicans have seized as an example of their economic powerlessness. Only 30% of the work force is Corsican, (as against 90% in 1960), and mainlanders are employed in exceptionally high numbers in banks (78%), and the Post, Education and Electricity Services.

In 1972, the Hudson Institute produced a secret report which the ARC discovered and leaked, which made recommendations for the future expansion of the tourist industry based on the import of more non-Corsicans. This, and a particular case of pollution of Corsican waters and beaches with chemicals from an Italian subsidiary of Montedison, added to the separatists' and autonomists' anger, and attracted the attention of the French government. During a visit in 1974, the then Prime Minister said he would crush 'without pity' any violent attempts at separatism, but he went on to make some concessions to Corsican feelings, by establishing a cheaper transport system to the mainland (imports made the cost of living 30% higher than the mainland), promising the establishment of a University (under Paoli, one had been established, as had a mint, and a press) and cheaper agricultural land to Corsican farmers. Corsican demands extend to the removal of the foreign legion posts at Calvi, Bonifacio and Corte, the expulsion of the *colons* and re-distribution of land, with a reversion to self-sufficient agriculture; and an increased 'Corsicasation' of tourism, banking, industry etc. at all levels. Most would be content to leave Foreign Affairs and Defence to Paris, but extremists require complete separation. Concessions will be required from both sides, if the sense of injustice, and acts of violence and repression are not to increase beyond control.

G.A.

SELECT BIBLIOGRAPHY

Gregori, J., *Nouvelle Histoire de la Corse,* Editions Jerome Martineau, Paris, 1967
Heraud, G., *L'Europe des Ethnies,* Presses d'Europe, Paris, 1974
Leoni, G., *Corsica: 9000 Ans d'Histoire,* Editions Presenza Corsa
Simeoni, E., *Le Piege d'Aleria,* Editions Lattes, 1975
Stephens, Marc, *Linguistic Minorities in Western Europe,* Gomer Press, 1976
Stevanu et al, *Les Temps Modernes,* Paris, April 1976

18   Dominica's Carib Indians

Dominica, an island of 305 square miles, is the third largest of the British group of West Indian Islands, with a population of 75,000. A Crown Colony since 1805, Dominica became a British-Associated State in 1967. The last Carib Indians live today in a reserved territory of 37,000 acres known as Salybia accessible only by foot or Land Rover. Estimates vary, but out of about 19,000 people on the Reserve, only some 70 are pure Carib, another 300 largely Carib, and the rest are at least half Negro.

The Caribs were originally a branch of the Galibi Indians of Guyana. In about 1200 AD large bands of Caribs sailed to the West Indies in their 60' dugout canoes, leaving their women behind, killing the Arawak men, and taking the Arawak women as their own. According to Spanish writers of the 16th century, the Carib nation extended from the Virgin Islands, east of Puerto Rico, to the mouth of the Amazon.

In 1493 Columbus planted the flag of Spain on Dominica, but his stay was short-lived, as the Caribs drove him and his men off with poisoned arrows, and for 200 years the Caribs kept European colonists away from Dominica. Indeed the island was declared neutral in 1748 by the Treaty of Aix-la-Chapelle, and left to the Caribs. It was well into the 17th century before the French missionaries made contact with them, but failed to make many converts. With the decline of Spain as a colonial power, throughout the 18th century France and England disputed possession of this fertile, well-watered island. At first the French dominated, and in spite of the provisions of the Aix-la-Chapelle treaty, French settlers moved in to cultivate the rich soil. Then in 1759 the English captured Dominica, and British possession was formally recognised by the Treaty of Paris in 1763, and again by the Treaty of Versailles. In 1769, Britain allowed French settlers to stay on the island on payment of a quit rent. The rest of the cultivable land was sold to English settlers. The Caribs, however, driven north into the least accessible areas were allotted all of 134 acres by Queen Charlotte, without legal title. By 1798, 15,000 slaves had been imported in chains from Africa to work the settlers' plantations.

In 1880 an American explorer wrote that the Carib 'has been almost civilised out of existence'. More to the point, the Carib had been virtually exterminated by 1900. In 1903 the British Administrator, Sir Hesketh Bell, 'gave' the Caribs their present Reserve, without legal title, or any mention of their rights or privileges. When Dominica was made a State in Association with Britain in 1967, the Caribs had no say about this arrangement.

Traditionally the Caribs are hunters and sailors, living chiefly by fishing in the rivers and the sea, and hunting manicou and agouti in the forests with mute dogs. Formerly self-sufficient, they now devote themselves more to the production of articles for sale or in exchange for European goods, and less to traditional crafts. They earn a livelihood mainly by fishing for freshwater crayfish, boniques, dorades and tuna, making traditional baskets and dugout canoes from gommier trees. (The English word 'canoe' is derived from the original Carib 'Kanawa'). Some have resorted to agricultural labour on the plantations outside the Reserve. Most communal projects died with the matrilocal joint family (although young couples often live with the girl's parents before or after marriage). It is still thought by some elder Caribs that a child inherits its 'blood' from his mother, and only its 'spirit' from its father.

Until World War I, the Caribs spoke three languages: the male Carib, the female Arawak, and the Council a secret language. Since then they have spoken a mixture of French Creole patois and English. They have always had an elected Chief, whose duties are, as leader, spokesman and delegate, to act and make decisions in the general interest of all Caribs. Prestige apart, he enjoys no special privileges, and acts together with a Council of five men. The Caribs are now no more formally organised than this, but their Chief plays an increasing role in their struggle for existence. For it is he who negotiates with the Dominican government.

Few Dominicans know much about the Caribs, and very few ever visit the Reserve. Besides its very considerable natural beauty, Dominica uses the Caribs as tourist attraction. There are still relatively few tourists, but unless the Caribs can sell them their baskets or demand money to be photographed, currency spent by the tourist does not filter back to the Reserve. There are few social services available to the Caribs, partly because of their inaccessibility, and insufficient housing, transport, educational and medical facilities result. Carib children usually learn just enough at school to lose interest in traditional, tribal pursuits, but far too little to find new ones. While many other tribal groups are impoverished, exploited and alienated, the real Carib problem is whether or not they will become extinct in the immediate future. Argument centres round the legal title to Reserve land, and who shall be permitted to live on it. This battle for survival with the Dominican government has been deadlocked for several years.

Linda Barnard Finer

SELECT BIBLIOGRAPHY

Jesse, Rev. C., *The Carib,* Journal of the Barbados Museum and Historical Society, Bridgetown, February 1960

Lowenthal, D., *West Indian Societies,* Institute of Race Relations, Oxford University Press, London, 1972

Ober, F.A., *Camps in the Caribbees,* Boston, 1880

Ober, F.A., *Aborigines of the West Indies,* Worcester, Mass. 1894

Rouse, I., *The Carib,* Handbook of South American Indians, Washington DC, 1948

Smith, M.G., *The Plural Societies of the British West Indies,* University of California, Berkeley, 1965

19 The Estonians

The Estonians are a Finno-Ugrian people, whose language is closely related to Finnish. Their territory is on the Baltic coast, north of Latvia and west of Leningrad. They were under the colonial rule of Germans, Danes, Swedes and Russians for 700 years.

In the 13th century, the Estonians were colonised partly by the German knight order, the Brethren of the Sword, and partly by the Danes under King Valdemar II. North Estonia, with its strategic ports on the Baltic, Tallin and Narva, became a Danish colony, while South Estonia was added to the territory of the German knightly orders in Latvia. In the 14th century, the Order of Teutonic Knights took over the whole of Estonia. In 1558 Estonia was invaded by the Muscovites under Ivan the Terrible, and became the theatre of war between the Swedes and Russians. In 1582, the country was largely colonised by Sweden and was fully annexed by the Swedish King Gustavus Adolphus II in

1625. Under the Swedes, the peasants were granted fuller rights and legal redress than had been the case under the feudal system imposed by the German knightly orders. The Baltic German nobility therefore cooperated with the Russian take-over of Estonia in 1704–10 under Tsar Peter the Great. Their reward was a restoration of Baltic German landed estates and feudal rights over the Estonian peasantry. The local government became a Baltic German monopoly under the Tsarist Russian bureaucracy. The Estonian peasants were formally freed from serfdom in 1816–19, but landowners retained various privileges over the peasantry until 1868.

The Estonian national and political movement in education and literature also dates from the 1860's. It combined the struggle against Russification with the fight against social injustice. The Estonian national movement contributed to the revolutionary disturbances of 1905 and the greater Estonian participation in local government that followed. After the Russian Revolution of 1917 the Estonian national leaders called for autonomous self-government, the principle of which was granted in April 1917 by the Provisional Government. After the Bolshevik revolution of October 1917 the Estonian National Council, made up of members of elected parties, decided to break away from the Russian state on 28 November 1917, while independence was formally declared on 24 February 1918. In November 1918 Soviet Russian armies invaded Estonia but were repulsed after a short campaign. White Russian and German forces operating inside Estonia were also disbanded. In 1920, a peace treaty was signed with the Soviet government, in which Russia renounced 'forever' her sovereign rights over the territory and people of Estonia. An independent, elected government of Estonians ruled the country until 1940, when Estonia was invaded by the Soviet Union under the terms of the German-Soviet pact.

After the Soviet take-over, the 'elections' took place in the same way as in the other Baltic republics and Estonia was incorporated into the Soviet Union on 4 August 1940. During 1940–41 58,037 Estonians were deported to remote areas of the Soviet Union and 1,950 were killed in Soviet Estonian prisons.

The Soviet invasion was followed in 1941 by a German invasion and occupation which lasted until 1944. In 1944 the country was re-occupied by Soviet forces and was re-organized on the Soviet model. All farming land, formerly the property of small farmers, was collectivized and opponents of this policy were deported to labour camps or exiled. The numbers deported from Estonia to labour camps in the Soviet Union in 1944–56 were roughly double the number deported in 1940–41.

The present population of Estonia is 1,428,000 (1975). Of these, 68.2% are Estonian by nationality, compared with 88.2% in 1935. 24.7% of the population are Russians. The increase in the country's population since 1939, (when it was just over 1 million), is largely due to Russian immigration into Estonian towns, in combination with the emigration of 80,000 Estonians to the West in 1944. Between 1951 and 1960, 47.8% of population increase was due to immigration, while in the years 1959–70 this percentage rose to 61%. In some post-war industries, such as the shale oil refinery in Narva, the majority of employees are non-Estonians. As in Latvia, immigrants from Russia are attracted by the higher living standards and the demand for labour of the large and growing industrial sector.

Only 12.5% of Russians in Estonia are fluent in Estonian, but in contrast to the situation in Latvia, Estonians are largely refusing to adopt Russian as a second language: only 27.5% of Estonians speak Russian fluently, and it has been noticed by foreign tourists in Tallinn that Estonians will often refuse to answer if spoken to in Russian. 74% of books and journals published in Estonia are in Estonian. 22% of marriages are between Estonians and Russians, while 13.6% of all families are linguistically mixed. 62% of teenagers in such families considered themselves Estonian, according to a Soviet survey carried out in the 1960s.

Only 52.3% of the Estonian Communist Party are Estonians (1970), while Russians constitute 36.9% of its membership. Since a party card is a pre-requisite for appointment to most positions of authority in the government and civil service it can be assumed that Russians hold an equally disproportionate percentage of positions of influence in Estonia. The Estonian Communist Party has had the same problems of 'national Communism' as the Latvian Party; in 1949–51 Nikolai Karotamm, First Secretary of the Estonian Party Central Committee, made some attempts to resist Russification, particularly in schools, and to protect Estonian national traditions. He was removed from office, together with those who supported him. The present First Secretary, Ivan Kabin, spent his formative years in Russia and is much more Russian-orientated. However 'national Communism' is obviously not dead in Estonian Party circles: in 1972, Artur Vader, Chairman of the Praesidium of the Estonian Supreme Soviet, publicly attacked the idea that Estonia should separate itself from the Soviet Union, while remaining a socialist state. Although Vader attributed this point of view to Estonian emigres, the very prominence given to the statement and the fact that independence is linked with socialism make it very probable that the attack is aimed at certain socialist circles in Estonia itself. The idea of 'socialism with a human face' has been influential in Estonia, as in other East European countries: in 1968, some members of the technical intelligentsia in Estonia compiled an appeal calling for the democratization of Soviet society, freedom of the press and of political activity and liberation for all political prisoners.

Other groups, more interested in national independence as such, also exist, as is known from underground 'samizdat' publications. In 1969, a memorandum compiled by Baltic, Russian and Ukrainian democrats called for the implementation of every nation's right to secede from the Soviet Union. The Russian-language dissident journal, 'The Chronicle of Current Events', No. 25, (1972), reported the existence of an 'Estonian National Front', whose programme included self-determination for Estonia; it also noted the existence of an Estonian samizdat journal — 'The Estonian Democrat'. In 1974, an appeal from two groups — the Estonian National Front and the Estonian Democratic Movement — was sent to Kurt Waldheim, Secretary-General of the United Nations, demanding 'the restoration of independence and basic human rights to the Estonian nation'; it also called for the evacuation of Soviet troops and the holding of free elections. In June 1975, a declaration by Estonian and Latvian democrats called for the implementation of the human rights and freedoms laid down in the United Nations Charter and the Declaration of Human Rights.

Recently, in October 1975, five dissidents — three Estonians (Mattik, Kiirend and Varato), one Russian Estonian (Soldatov) and a Ukrainian (Yuskevich) — were tried in Tallinn, for writing a letter to the United Nations asking for the restoration of national and human rights in Estonia. They are believed to have been closely linked with the Estonian Democratic Movement. Mattik and Soldatov were sentenced to 6 years in strict regime labour camps while Kiirend and Yuskevich were sentenced to 5 years in similar camps. Varato turned state's evidence and got a suspended sentence. The sentences will be served in camps outside Estonia.

In spite of Russian immigration figures and the Soviet government's Russification policy, Estonian national morale is generally high. This may be partly due to their close ties with Finland. A large number of tourists from Finland take their holidays in Estonia every year; Finnish radio and television programmes can often be obtained on Estonian sets. As Finnish is linguistically close to Estonian, the Estonians probably feel more in touch with the West than some of the other minority nationalities of the Soviet Union.

Marite Sapiets

SELECT BIBLIOGRAPHY

Baltic Events, Nos 1–2, February–April 1974, Irvine, California
Chronicle of Current Events, Nos. 7, 11, 24, 25, Khronika Press, New York
Isupov, A., *Nationalny Sostav Naseleniya SSR,* Moscow, 1961
Itogi Vsesoyuznoi Perepisi Naseleniya 1970, Moscow, 1973
Narodnoye Khozyaistvo Estonskoi SSR v 1972, Tallinn, 1973
Parming, T., *The Social Consequences of Population Changes in Estonia since 1939,* Acta Baltica, No. 11, 1972
Raud, V., *Estonia,* New York, 1953
Soviet Analyst, 3, No. 21, October 1974; 3, No. 9, April 1975
Vader, A., *The Estonian Socialist Nation as an Organic Part of the New Historic Community of Peoples,* Kommunist Estonii, No. 5, 1972
Vardys, V.S., *The Baltic Peoples,* Problems of Communism, September–October 1967
Vardys, V.S., *Modernisation and Baltic Nationality,* Problems of Communism, September–October 1975

20 The Galicians

Not much is known about the original inhabitants of north western Spain. Many invasions inevitably occurred in this peninsula within a peninsula: present day Galicia was infiltrated in time by Celts, Phoenicians, Greeks and Suevis, and provided a bastion against the Roman invasion. Later, the remote mountains, numerous *rias,* and climatic instability, provided a haven for many other Spanish inhabitants who fled from the eighth century onslaught of the Moors, and thus Galicia developed a marked independence while much of the rest of Spain was dominated by the Moors.

Galicia both enjoys and resents its all-important geographical separation. In common with other Celtic minorities, it enjoys its distinctive history, language and culture; it resents its present lack of privileges. The claims of the Galicians to some kind of independent status unlike those of the Basques or Catalans, rests more vaguely, more romantically, yet more ineradicably on substantial cultural differences which have permeated the life style of its inhabitants and influenced their goals. These claims may still be more theoretically than practically based as the logical product of the memories of the glorious past mixing with the discomfort of the present.

In the literary sphere Galicia was once Spain's inspiration: the expression of the Spanish essence of being. A school of lyric poetry in Galicia, with its centre in Santiago, was created a century before the birth of Chaucer, to become the chief poetic form throughout Spain for at least two centuries, and influence of many different artists later. Its indigenous character, usually in quatrain, is thought to link it firmly with the Celtic. On the themes of nature and love, retaining a peasant simplicity even earthiness, a pure lyrical quality co-existed and developed alongside with much more sophisticated elements. Gallegan became the language of a cultivated elite, an essential attribute for the educated vanguard throughout that period.

The music and songs of Galicia are also important. In common with the Bretons, the Scots and the Irish, the Galicians have their own bagpipes — called *gaitas* — as well as the more usual tambourines and drums. These are used, together with the traditional dances, to mark all the historic festivals. These are Songs for the New Year, for the Day of Kings, for May, for courting, and for multitudinous religious celebrations.

In religious, as in racial terms, the Galicians are a strange and old mixture with one distinctive theme — the theme of souls — as their constant point of reference. Old pagan traditions have survived hardily by the side of the great Christian pilgrimage centre in their midst — Santiago de Compostella. Despite the fact that Galicia and Asturias were the places where Christianity took refuge from the Moors, the deep-rooted Celtic type of subculture appears still as a top layer. A rosary for souls is said with the evening Angelus, Galician beggars plead for offerings on behalf of the souls (*Séa por las animas*), and often tables are laid for the souls alongside of those for the more visible, or food is left out at night or offered on actual tombs to appease potential tormentors. These rituals run concurrently with the preservation of belief in black and white magic, the evil eye, witchcraft, and the powers of some herbs. Although funeral rites are of supreme importance in Galicia they do not have a distancing effect but rather contribute to the overall aim of keeping the dead on as silent but real members of the community. The Galicians have an easy sense of familiarity with death and they bury their dead in the same place as they dance, have fiestas, and work. Needs, wants, and feelings are attributed to the Galician dead as a means of communication both with them and with the *edad de oro situada mas alla del bien y del mal.*

Paradoxically enough it was in the heart of this inaccessible region of peasants and poets that the body of the apostle St. James was discovered in the ninth century. Santiago de Compostella became the religious capital of Europe, the Mecca of the West. Thousands flocked to 'Sent James in Galiz' and the pilgrims were almost a logical extension of the invaders in that they upheld the cosmopolitan past bringing many foreign offerings as well as a continual influx of ideas. The pilgrimage to Santiago acquired great prestige and easily rivalled Rome and Jerusalem since Spain was, in the early stages, ruled largely by the Moors. Santiago has provided a link with the outside world, and remains a town of great character and beauty of which the Galicians are rightly proud.

Galician daily life is different from that of Castile, Catalonia, the Basque country or any other Spanish region. The changeable and often rainy weather ensures that the Galician home has a more practical domestic significance than elsewhere. The women here are more active and more dominant than is customary in Spain and they often do 'a man's work' from sheer necessity as the majority of men emigrate for part of their lives. Emigration is a tradition and a necessity, dictated by over-division of the land among 'tiny proprietors', bedevilled by numerous territorial squabbles and lawsuits. Although Galicia has such an important coastline, it does not contain enough work for its own population. The central government effectively exploits Galician resources without improving communications, without aiding agriculture to any extent, and without encouraging the small native industries such as pottery, lace-making and sandal and clog production. The standard of living is the lowest anywhere in Spain, but, as the old saying goes, 'Galicia is rich, it is we *Gallegos* who are poor'.

The dreaminess and gentle romanticism associated with the Galicians, and the lack of political substance in their ideas and aims, doubles their present predicament. The low key campaign to have Gallegan re-instated as a language of culture and erudition rather than keeping it as the tongue of the lower classes is likely to be overlooked by Madrid. The separatist party is neither very strong nor very united since a substantial proportion of the more active Galicians are abroad and Galicia is not in itself a united ethnic unity. Its customs, dress and language vary as much as its dramatic scenery. It is ironic that the very people who would be best suited to furthering the Galician cause are forced to work in alien climes because of sheer economic deprivation. The examples of the Catalans and the Basques may be taken and built upon, but it seems that neither consciousness nor coherent organisation will reach that stage for some time yet.

Catherine Akester

SELECT BIBLIOGRAPHY

Bell, A., *Spanish Galicia*, London, 1922
Martinez-Barbeito, C., *Galicia Destino*, Barcelona, 1965

Epton, N., *Spain's Magic Coast,* Weidenfeld and Nicholson, London, 1965

Madariaga, S. de, *Spain: A Modern History,* Jonathan Cape, London, 1961

Rodriguez y Rodriguez, *Fisonomia y alma de Galicia,* Aguirre, Madrid, 1955

Starkie, W., *The Road to Santiago,* Murray, London, 1958

Walles, *Spain: The Gentle Anarchy,* Pall Mall Press, London, 1965

21 The Georgians

Transcaucasia, which includes the three Soviet Socialist Republics (SSR's) of Georgia, Armenia and Azerbaidzhan is a region of dense population and extraordinary ethnic diversity, containing at least 50 distinct peoples each with their own language and traditions, but having more in common with each other than with their Russian neighbours to the north. The Georgians, who call themselves 'Kartveli', and their country 'Sakartvelo', (both names deriving from 'Kartli', the central province in which the capital Tbilisi is situated) are culturally, economically and numerically the most important nationality of the region with perhaps a stronger sense of national identity than any of their neighbours.

Georgia had a total population of 4,878,000 in 1974. A previous census broke it down as follows: Georgians 3,130,741 (66.8%); Armenians 452,309 (9.7%); Russians 396,694 (8.5%); Azerbaidzhanis 217,758 (4.6%); Greeks (1.9%); Jews (1.1%); and other minorities, such as the Ossets (3.2%); Abkhaz (1.79%); and Adzhars (Georgian Moslems), who are mainly concentrated in their respective Autonomous Regions. Despite Georgian fears of Russification some of the smaller nationalities, such as the Abkhaz, are gradually being assimilated by the Georgians themselves. 90,000 Georgians live outside Georgia within the U.S.S.R., some tens of thousands in northern Iran and an estimated 300,000 Georgians and Lazes (a related people) in Turkey: there is also a small Georgian emigré colony in Paris. It should be noted that the concentration of Georgians living in their own republic (96.5% in 1970), is higher than that of any other Soviet nationality.

Occupying a key position between East and West, Georgia has a long and turbulent history. Christianity was accepted as the official religion almost six centuries before Russia; Georgia came under Persian, Arab, Seljuk and Mongol hegemony over the Bagratid dynasty which ruled for a thousand years until it was annexed by the Russians. It reached a political, economic and cultural apogee under the Golden Age of Queen Tamara (1184–1213) from which period much of Georgia's finest art, church-architecture and literature dates. Georgia turned to Orthodox Russia, which by now extended almost as far south as the Caucasus, for protection against Ottoman Turkey and Safavi Persia, and in 1783 a treaty of friendship was signed. Annexation followed in 1801. The Georgian nobility received the same privileges as the Russian, but in 1811 the Georgian Orthodox Church, traditionally a focus of opposition to foreign rule, was incorporated into the Russian Orthodox Church.

Discontent with the Russian administration led to a peasant revolt in 1812, and an abortive attempt to restore the old monarchy in 1832. Renewed contact with Europe generated some positive social and economic developments, and the first Georgian language newspaper. The lot of the peasants, however, failed to improve, even after the emancipation of 1864–71, and as the population increased the pressure on land became acute. The new liberal intelligensia, educated at Russian universities, grew increasingly critical of the Tsarist autocracy, campaigning against serfdom, and calling for radical reform. The Russian administration pursued a policy of Russification, banning the Georgian language from educational establishments in 1871–2. The most influential political movement in pre-revolutionary Georgia was the Marxist Third Group (Mesame Dasi), founded in 1892; its members included Nikolai Chkheidze, future Menshevik president of the Petrograd Soviet in 1917, Noe Zhordania who was to become president of independent Georgia, and Josef Dzhugashvili, the future Stalin.

The discontent which spread from the countryside to the towns, provoking serious unrest, before the First World War, when Georgia was the scene of fighting against the Turks. The Mensheviks came to power following the abdication of Nicholas

II, and the October 1917 Revolution pledging allegiance to the Russian Provisional Government, but after the Treaty of Brest-Litovsk, Georgia declared her independence, which was recognised by twenty-two countries including Britain and Soviet Russia in 1920. Having concluded alliances with Germany and Britain, the government embarked on a programme of socialist reform.

On the pretext of supporting a popular uprising, the Red Army invaded Georgia early in 1921, placing it under Communist rule. The former Menshevik government fled to the West, while the remaining party members were liquidated on Stalin's orders. The Georgian Catholics Patriarch was imprisoned, and the Bolsheviks' heavy-handed action exacerbated the political differences between Lenin and Stalin who, as Commissar for Nationalities, had been largely responsible for it. Despite strong opposition from the Georgian Communist leaders, Stalin successfully advocated a federal policy and in 1922 Georgia entered the U.S.S.R. as part of the Transcaucasian Socialist Federated Soviet Republic (SFSR) together with Armenia and Azerbaidzhan. An anti-communist insurrection in 1924 was ruthlessly crushed.

Under Stalin, who all his life spoke Russian with a Georgian accent, Georgians occupied some of the most important positions in the U.S.S.R. (including Beria, second only to Stalin himself) but while making considerable economic and social progress, Georgia suffered badly in Stalin's purges which reached their height in 1936–7, removing any possibility of opposition from the Communist Party, the security forces or the intellectuals. During 1926–39 there was a great influx of Russians into Georgia: agriculture was collectivised, industrialisation proceeded apace, and the living standards of the workers and peasants at last began to rise. The Transcaucasian SFSR lasted until 1936, when the Georgian SSR was created.

During the Second World War Georgia was again threatened by the rapid German advance through southern Russia in 1941–2, but the Red Army prevented further penetration from the North Caucasus. Manifestations of unrest, particularly in some mountainous areas, though far less serious than in the Ukraine, gave the authorities disquiet and on Stalin's orders several minorities were deported. At the end of the war, the allied agreement of 1945–6 resulted in the forcible repatriation of thousands of Georgians, many of whom were then shot or exiled to Siberia.

After Stalin's death in 1953, the new first secretary of the CPG, Nzhavanadze, rehabilitated many Georgian writers and scientists, and in 1956 Krushchev made his famous 'secret speech' denouncing Stalin's crimes. Georgia's post-war recovery was not only economic but also social, cultural and to some extent, political. De-Stalinisation had some unforeseen consequences in Georgia: on the third anniversary of the death of the 'great son of the Georgian nation' (3rd March 1956), serious riots occurred in Tbilisi, involving, surprisingly for the U.S.S.R., students. 106 people are said to have been killed and over 200 wounded and several hundred subsequently deported to Siberia.

Mzhavanadze kept a tight reign on Georgian nationalism and the Orthodox Church, but overlooked the problem of bribery and corruption, which spread to the highest levels of his administration; private enterprise and speculation were officially ignored and the republic became the centre of a flourishing black market. This led to his replacement in 1972, by Shevardnadze, former Minister of Internal Security. In an attempt to eliminate corruption and bureaucratic inefficiency, Shevardnadze began an extensive purge of the administration; within two years some 25,000 people had been arrested, including Communist Party and Komsomol (Young Communist League) parties, and police and KGB employees.

Today, Georgian nationalism is expressed more in a legitimate (sometimes perhaps excessive) pride in Georgia's ancient and unique language and culture and in her many and varied achievements, not least during the Soviet period, than in political demands for greater autonomy or even full independence, which is, at least theoretically, possible under Article 17 of the Soviet Constitution. In recent years there has been a growing demand for the full observance of basic human rights and civil liberties supposedly guaranteed by the Civil Code of the GSSR, the Constitution of the U.S.S.R., and by the United Nations Declaration of Human Rights. Georgia's tradition of providing outstanding Soviet leaders has been maintained, and her achievements in a variety of fields from science to sport are remarkable for so small a people, but are perhaps most impressive in the arts.

Nationalism is also expressed in the preservation of a

distinctive way of life in which wine, food, music, dancing, open-air cafes and sport play an important part. Individualistic, flamboyant in gesture, hostile to all forms of regimentation, Georgians are even more hospitable than the Russians, and they probably have more in common with the peoples of the Mediterranean. The GSSR ranks first in the national composition of the CPSU, first in its level of higher and secondary education, first in the average size of savings account.

It is difficult to assess the current strength of the Georgian Orthodox Church traditionally an opponent of outside rule. Various sources suggest that the authorities are seriously concerned about its influence on young people despite what many would regard as an official campaign to discredit it. The theft of valuables from the Patriarchate in 1972 provoked a scandal. Documents tell of an astonishing story of corruption in the hierarchy and of courageous efforts to combat it, indicting the present Patriarch of Georgia and the Bishop of Tsilkanskaya. The latter is portrayed as being guilty of gross immorality and criminality and as being a conscious agent of the KGB. The Georgian Orthodox Church appears, however, to have about 40 working churches although before the Revolution there were some 2000 parishes. It was severely persecuted in the 1920s, as a leader of Georgian national resistance to Soviet rule. It is not known what proportion of the population go to church. The only seminary was reported, in the late 1960s, to have 10 students (before the Revolution there were 400 seminarians) and educational standards are said to be low.

A significant development was the formation in 1974 of the Tbilisi Initiative Group for Human Rights by Dr. Zviad Gamsakhurdia, a Christian and a scholar, and at that time teacher of English and American literature at Tbilisi University. He also edits the only known samizdat literary journal in Georgian, 'The Golden Fleece', which first appeared in May 1975. Its declared aim is to publish stories, poems and articles which could not appear in the official press because of the ideological censorship. He has been subjected to a campaign of harrassment by the KGB, threats, searches, intimidation and, in July 1975, dismissal from his post at Tbilisi University.

Although some new education measures are alleged to be a step towards Russification, they may be better understood when seen in the wider context of the Soviet Union, whose only common language is Russian. Of the 4258 general education schools in the GSSR, in 1965–6, 2962 used Georgian as the language of instruction, 287 used Russian, 242 Armenian, 194 Ossetian, 162 Azerbaidzhani, 39 Abkhaz and 372 were bilingual. Georgian is reportedly often used as the language of instruction at higher and even technical schools which are largely Russified in the other republics. Fewer Georgians (only 21–25%) claimed to have a working knowledge of Russian than any other Soviet nationality in the 1970 census. Georgian is not only the mother tongue of the Georgians but is in fact accepted as the official language of the GSSR.

Finally, it should be emphasised that the Georgians suffer no more discrimination on the grounds of nationality than any other major national group in the U.S.S.R. While the pressures on their language and culture seem likely to increase rather than diminish, and the effects of recent administrative measures remain to be seen, the Georgians have resisted attempts at Russification, real or imagined, more successfuly than perhaps any other Soviet nationality.

Peter Hodges

SELECT BIBLIOGRAPHY

Allen, W.E.D., *A History of the Georgian People,* Kegan Paul, 1932
Davitaya, F.F., *Soviet Georgia,* Moseour, 1972
Gugushvili, P.N., *Gruzinskaya SSR,* Tbilisi, 1971
ed. Z. Katz et al, *A Handbook of Major Soviet Nationalities,* New York, 1975
Lang, D.M., *The Georgians,* Thames and Hudson, 1966
Lang, D.M., *A Modern History of Georgia,* Weidenfeld and Nicholson, 1962
A Chronicle of Current Events Nos. 32–33 translated and published in English by Amnesty International, 1976

22 Ghana: Ethnicity and Conflict Avoidance

Although significant geoethnic differences are apparent in modern Ghanaian society, successive regimes (with the obvious exception of Dr. K.A. Busia's short-lived administration) have chosen to play down, even to deny, the reality of these persisting cleavages. Despite this predisposition for conflict avoidance, Ghanaian observers themselves have commented that '. . . it should be clear to any Ghanaian that tribal discrimination is rampant in this country'. Tribalism is the 'natural bedfellow' of bribery and corruption; unless it was eliminated national unity would 'remain a dream'. Recruitment to positions would be determined by family or tribal ties, not by merit, and wealth would be distributed unfairly among groups and sub-regions. This may seem something of an over-statement yet it affords an insight into the critical part played by ethnicity on the contemporary Ghanaian scene.

The numerical proportions of major groups in the country and their dominance in the various sub-regions, and certain economic and social disparities as among these peoples are important. The data in the 1960 Census of Ghana are used, for although a subsequent survey was carried out in 1970 it provided a less complete guide.

In 1960 Ghana had a total population of 6,727,000 divided in the major groupings as follows: Akan 2,965,000 (44.1%); Mole-Dagbani, 1,072,000 (15.9%); Ewe, 876,000 (13.0%); Ga-Adangbe, 560,000 (8.3%); Guan, 252,000 (3.7%); Gurma, 238,000 (3.5%); Grusi, 148,000 (2.2%); Central Togo Tribes, 57,000 (0.8%); Tem, 51,000 (0.8%); Others, 508,000 (7.6%). When these aggregate ethnic populations are distributed on a sub-regional basis, the dominance of an ethnic (or ethnic sub-group) in each of these political sub-units becomes readily apparent. Thus sub-regionalism and ethnicity proved overlapping phenomena frequently being treated as indistinguishable in terms of identity.

When religion is cross-tabulated against ethnic group allegiance, a striking contrast emerges between southern and northern-based peoples. Among adults of both sexes, the percentage of members identifying themselves as Christians was 62.7% among the Akan, 54.5% among the Ga-Adangbe, 48.3% among the Ewe, 43.3% among the Guan and 71.4% among the Central Togo Tribes; however, among the northern peoples the percentage of Christian adherents was uniformly low, and those identifying themselves as Moslems were as follows: Mole-Dagbani, 21.9%; Grusi, 14.2%; Gurma, 20.9%; and the Tem, 96.6%. A significant proportion remain followers of traditional religions or, in some cases, no religion at all.

Significant differences by ethnic group also appeared with respect to adult literacy. The predominantly southern peoples contrast with their northern neighbours by their generally higher levels of literacy. Although current trends in school attendance seem likely to bring about some evening in these disparities in years to come, noticeable differences by ethnic group are still evident.

Inter-ethnic differences are also apparent with respect to types of occupations and employers. Among males, the Central Togo Tribes, and such northern peoples as the Lobi, the Mole-Dagbani and the Grusi and such a partly northern people as the Gurma showed the highest percentage in agricultural pursuits; the Ewes and peoples of semi-foreign origin (Hausa, Yoruba, Ibo) were ranked most prominently among those classified as craftsmen, production process workers, miners and quarrymen; the Tem and semi-foreign workers had high proportions of workers engaged in sales, transport and communication, service, and sports; and the Ga-Adangbe, Akan, Central Togo Tribes, Guan, and Ewe held down the largest number of white collar positions (professional and technical, administrative, managerial and clerical). Although female workers differed significantly as to overall occupation distribution (higher proportions in the sales, transportation, and communication category and lower proportions in the craftsmen and white collar categories), they varied only slightly from the males within the occupation categories themselves. Some significant differences were evident among those classified as craftsmen and production process workers, however, as Grusi, Ga-Adangbe, Guan and Lobi women did rank relatively high in this regard. Another indication of inter-ethnic differences in the employment sector is the percentages of males aged 15 and over employed in the public and non-public sectors; here they range from 53.1% among the Ga and 44.2% among the Tem to 11.0% among the Boron, 13.4% among the Lobi, and 14.1% among the Ga-Adangbe. Other inter-ethnic variations could be shown with respect to urbanization, forms of marriage and access to amenities (as indicated by the related variable of sub-region), but the foregoing data should be sufficient to demonstrate that substantial socio-economic differences do in fact exist among major groups and sub-groups within Ghana.

Conflict avoidance is apparent in both the ordinances and the political strategies of successive Ghanaian military governments. These administrations (the National Liberation Council, 1966–1969, and National Redemption Council/Supreme Military Council, 1972 to the present day), have both tolerated a limited amount of political activity, permitting only a narrow scope for the open pursuit of ethnic 'interests'. And when the ethnic aspect did manage to become an issue for public speculation, as during the 1976 trial of eight persons (all Ewes accused of plotting to overthrow the government by unlawful means), General Kutu Acheampong, the Head of State, formally denied that ethnic considerations as such were involved in the affair and appealed to the public to desist from victimizing the members of any community.

Despite efforts by the two military governments to shun the ethnic issue, the stubborn facts of Ghanaian life have precluded full success in this endeavour. The ethnic composition of the NLC marked a sharp reversal from the pre-coup Nkrumah experience. Whereas the proportion of Akans in the Nkrumah cabinet came to 69%, that for the NLC was a mere 25%. Then during the Busia interlude the proportion of Akans rose to a high of 74%, only to fall again to 60% in the period after the second military takeover. Obviously military coups brought significant shuffles in ethnic representation to the top-most level. The coming to power of the NLC signalled a shift, in military as well as civilian appointments, away from Akan hegemony. Similarly the NRC coup of 1972 brought together a mixed group of army officers: the leaders — Lt. Col. I.K. Acheampong (Asante), Major K. Baah (Boron), Major A. Selormey (Ewe), and Major K.G. Agbo (Ewe) — reflected a change of emphasis from the imbalances of the Busia period. 'Friendships based on career patterns were more important (at least in 1972) than ethnic considerations, but it is also true that many Ewe officers felt that they had been badly treated by the Busia Government.' comments Valerie Plave Bennett on this military take-over. It is interesting that since that time the Acheampong regime has maintained a rough equivalence between Akans and non-Akans in the cabinet. Moreover this regime has been highly attentive to the ethnic factor in its appointment of regional commissioners. As of November 1975, the NRC administration could boast that five out of nine regional commissioners hailed from their own units, this represents the highest proportion of regional commissioners from their own area in many years.

Inevitably, budgetary allocation patterns also embroiled the military in inter-ethnic and inter-regional encounters. Even while expressing dissatisfaction with the economic policies of both civilian regimes and promising programmes of rural development, the military regimes have had little redistributive impact upon expenditure patterns. The NLC, in comparison to the Nkrumah regime, reduced allocations for such economically productive sectors as industry, agriculture, trade and communications while increasing those for defence and foreign affairs. Although NRC/SMC priorities seem less skewed, a comparison with expenditures under the Busia regime (prior to 13 January 1972) revealed little tendency to spend a greater percentage of resources on productive or social welfare activities. It is instructive to note the priorities Colonel Acheampong announced shortly after assuming office. He declared the country to be 'on the verge of bankruptcy' and asserted 'We must endeavour to increase savings, and mobilise all available domestic resources'. The solution, in terms of hinterland development, involved an emphasis upon agricultural improvement and diversification on the one hand but a reduction in feeder road construction and a suspension of the rural electrification scheme on the other. Resource scarcity thus gave rise to irresolution on rural deprivation. Thus, as was the case with recruitment practices, the army regimes necessarily affected ethnic interests variously in the way that they allocated expenditure on rural or urban-linked activities. The salience of ethnicity made impossible a full and effective posture of conflict avoidance — particularly in an environment of evident and increased scarcity.

As a consequence, public policies on recruitment and resource allocation take on a political significance of the first order; where ethnic groups on the periphery regard themselves as relatively disadvantaged, they come to question the legitimacy of government, and sometimes the political order itself. It is this sense of relative deprivation, and the resulting doubts on regime legitimacy, which makes the ethnic issue such a crisis-laden one in current Ghanaian circumstances. And the proclivity of governments to deny conflict lends an aspect of 'incoherence' to already ineffective linkages between centre and periphery. Thus the command element in military government becomes coterminous with conflict avoidance, making for a communications void and lack of systematized relations essential to effective conflict reduction.

In Ghana today, this combination of circumstances is nowhere more evident than in the Ewe secessionist movement. Moreover it illustrates Milton M. Gordon's point that 'the degree of access to societal rewards . . . available to the minority ethnic group affects the degree of felt dissatisfaction of the group and thus affects the dynamics of social change with determine the outcome at any given time.' Ewe dissatisfaction seems inexplicable unless seen against a backdrop of increasing anxiety over access to public resources and opportunities, and as Ewe dissatisfaction has increased, it has created a momentum of its own which will not be satisfied by a minimal distribution of symbolic and material rewards.

A feeling, whether justified or not, that uneven development will become more and more apparent in the future causes some Ewes to despair and take desperate measures. In its extreme form, this sense of frustration finds expression in the advocacy of Volta Region secession and unification with Togo. That these sentiments are taken seriously in official quarters is evident from the Acheampong government's reaction. In March 1976, as tensions in Volta Region mounted, Ghanaian authorities banned the National Liberation Movement of Togoland, warned that they would defend against any aggression against their territory, and took steps to amend the Subversion Decree to include the advocacy, organisation or promotion of secession, or the breaking away of any part of Ghana from the territory of Ghana. Subsequently the police arrested ten people in Ho for alleged contacts with Ghanaians in exile in the Republic of Togo. Taking the offensive against secession, the SMC launched 'Operation Counter-Point', a part re-assertion of governmental determination to prevent secessionist inroads and a part reassurance on generous distributional policies in the future. In June, Brigadier R.E.A. Kotei, the Commissioner for Information, assured audiences in the Volta Region that progress in the area would be maintained through the provision of various amenities and services: *i.e.,* good roads, health facilities, education and clean drinking water. And some six weeks later, General Acheampong told a gathering at Ho that, in contradistinction to an openly-elected party government (with its continual airing of conflict and assumed parochial input), his administration was committed to the total and even development of the country. Relieved of the decisional costs of bargaining, it could, he apparently believed, impose a transformation of the economy from the top.

Certainly assurances of full access to societal rewards went to the source of much of current Ewe disaffection. Only through concerted efforts at corrective equity can the Acheampong regime hope to lay a solid foundation for coherent inter-ethnic relations. But is the military regime in a sound position from which to launch a transformationalist policy? In theory it possesses a monopoly of force and can command acceptance of its programme from the public at large. But in practice the articulate public outside the Volta Region, its main support base, seems unlikely to stand aside while a major shift in public allocation policies takes place. Resources for development remain scarce and competition for these resources in intense. Hence a predisposition toward conflict avoidance seems unlikely to mask the sharp cleavages among ethnic groups over the long term, and it seems certain to contribute little toward preparing for the kind of effective political linkages which seem indispensable to lasting national integration.

Donald Rothchild

SELECT BIBLIOGRAPHY

Austin, D., and Luckham, R., (eds.) *Politicians & Soldiers in Ghana 1966–72,* Frank Cass, London, 1975

Gil, B., Ayres, A.F., Ghansah, D.K., *1960 Population Census of Ghana, Specialist Report 'E', Tribes in Ghana,* Census Office, Accra, 1964

Glazer, N., and Moynihan, D.P., *Ethnicity: Theory and Experience,* Harvard University Press, Cambridge, Mass., 1975

Halpern, M., *Applying a New Theory of Human Relations to the Comparative Study of Racism,* University of Denver, Denver, 1969

Price, R.M., *A Theoretical Approach to Military Rule in New States: Reference Group Theory and the Ghanaian Case,* World Politics, 23, No. 3, April 1971

Rothchild, D., *Racial Bargaining in Independent Kenya: A Study of Minorities and Decolonisation,* Institute of Race Relations, Oxford University Press, London, 1973

Smock, D.R., A.C., *The Politics of Pluralism: A Comparative Study of Lebanon and Ghana,* Elsevier, New York, 1975

23   The Hill People of Northern Thailand

With the recent political changes in Thailand it is likely that the ambiguous position of the hill tribes will become increasingly important. Accurate statistics are difficult owing to their restiveness, but at present there are about 284,000 hill people centred in the north of Thailand, comprising various tribes. According to the Tribal Research Centre at Chiengmai University, there have been recent large influxes of Lahu people from Burma, saying they find Thailand more 'peaceful'.

The hill tribes may be broadly classified into three main racial types: those of Austronesian stock, who have migrated from the south (the Wa group), namely the Lawa (8,000), Kha Htin (23,200), Kha Mu (4,150), Kha Haw (200), and the elusive Yumbri (50?), regarded in popular belief as ghosts: and those of Sino-Tibetan stock (Mongoloid), who have migrated from the north. These latter may be divided into two main groups: the main Chinese (Yao-Meo-Peteng) group, including the Haw (600), recent refugees from China, many with Kuomintang affiliations, the Yao (20,000), and three tribes of the Meo people (40,800):

and the Lo Lo-Nosu (Tibeto-Burman) group, from which stem the Akha (9,900), the Lisu (10,500), four tribes of the Lahu (16,200), and four tribes of the Karen people (142,000). The latter two groups are thought to have originated from Yunnan and Kweichow provinces in China. The origins of the Wa are unclear, but it is possible, that they are of Polynesian-Micronesian stock.

The Yao-Meo-Pateng group speak a distinctive language of their own — a tonal language with faint Chinese influences. But the various tribes are not mutually intelligible one to another. The Haw speak Mandarin Chinese, and the Wa again have a distinctively separate language. However, various percentages of the tribes are proficient, in Shan, Burmese, Yunnanese, and the Lao-Thai northern dialect. There is no written form of language among the hill people, although some of the Yao use Chinese characters for their own language. Thai literacy is making headway owing to the Border Police school systems and missionary efforts. A missionary script is also in use among some Christianised hill people.

The religion of all the tribes is essentially animistic and shamanistic. They believe in good and evil spirits dwelling in all things. Many of them retain traces of Chinese practices in the forms of ancestor worship, exorcism, and animal sacrifice. A number have been converted to Christianity and Buddhism.

They are a nomadic people who are said to have originated from the Yellow River in China some 4,000 years ago, and to have migrated into Thailand during the past forty/fifty years from the neighbouring countries of Laos and Burma. They are still a nomadic people, and move with considerable freedom across the poorly patrolled borders of these countries.

However, it is in the interests of the Thai government to force them into a more settled mode of existence. This is because their mobility and extreme poverty makes them useful to Communist insurgents in the north of Thailand and elsewhere, who are able to supply them with badly needed commodities such as medicines, cigarettes and guns in return for services the most obvious of which is message-carrying. At present an unidentifiably large proportion of the hill people mantain a subsistence level of survival by growing opium, as they have done for centuries, and selling it on the black market. Consequently a settled mode of existence is out of the question: they move from place to place in the forest, are inaccessible and difficult to keep track of.

The Government has provided schools and health services in an attempt to reconcile the Meo and other tribes with Thai language and customs. Every evening a radio station broadcasts Thai news, commentaries, music and discussions in all dialects, there being on average one radio to one village. An intensive educational and housing programme has been set up aimed largely at persuading them to take up the growth of such innocent commodities as rice and maize, and which would ensure them leading a settled existence in the houses the Government is teaching them how to build. The scandal (and it is a well-known one in Thailand) is that the medicine and money and food which is provided by the Government often never gets delivered. Such is the state of corruption in Thai bureaucratic sectors that as these commodities pass through a long line of middlemen, some is inevitably kept back before being passed on, and when the remainder is finally due to be delivered to the hill people, government officials will often demand opium in exchange for the provisions, which they can then sell themselves on the black market. Despite the proclamations of the new military government, there is little hope that this will change.

The highest average yearly income per hill tribe family is 3,500Baht. for the northern Meo, whose main source of income is opium. This is excepting the newcome Haw, who make an average 10,000B a year per family from general trading. (3,500B is the equivalent of about £106 ($175) per family at present rates, and families are not nuclear, but in villages where thirteen or more people will live under the same roof.) The lowest figure quoted is that for the B'ghwe Karen, 500B (£15/$25). Later figures show no significant change from these, but it must be borne in mind that the people are, or were until recently, completely self-sufficient. The Akha remain completely self-sufficient today, still weaving their own cloth, and the Yumbri have never worried about a cash income because money is meaningless to them. Other tribes remain close to self-sufficiency.

The Meo, Yao, and Lisu are the tribes which rely mainly upon opium as their major source of income. Otherwise rice is grown for consumption, and maize as fodder for pigs and cattle. Sesame is cultivated for trade alone, chilli partly for trade and partly for consumption. Vegetables and fruit are grown in a small, unsystematic way around the houses — melon and cucumber, marrow and pumpkin, pineapples, bananas and papayas — as is common in Thailand. The people are most skilled in weaving, dyeing and embroidery, and their tribal clothes are particularly beautiful and striking. They are clever at woodcarving, making tables and crossbows, and basketware, and their music is also peculiarly fine.

Hygiene is a big problem: the people suffer from worms and skin infections, and malaria and malnutrition are common. Opium is in common use even in those places where it is not cultivated, for trade and consumption. The people regard themselves as the ancestors, not the dependants, of the Thai people. Shan was widely spoken, and there was a general determination to create a separate Shan state for themselves and other hill people in Burma. The situation, is further complicated by the hill people's various allegiances to the Laotian Communists (especially amongst the Meo), the Shan State Army in Burma, and the Thai government itself — to say nothing of the K settlements of the Haw Kuomintang that the Thai government has been unable to despatch to Taiwan.

It is not only the possibilities of insurgency and the prevalence of the opium trade which is causing the Thai government to take thought about the situation of the hill people, but also the slash-and-burn methods of (irrigationless) agriculture they employ. Large areas have been deforested by them, ten to twenty years being an average period for a hilltribe settlement, and so it is in the interests of the Thai government to ensure a more settled mode of existence for the hill people, based on more stable crops, and this necessitates the assimilation of the hill people into Thai culture, and the gradual loss of their identity. Tourism is another factor promoting this. The Police Border Patrol and NICOM (the Community Development Centre, part of the Public Welfare Department, which receives aid from the U.N.) are the two main agencies controlling this process. There is little doubt that under present policies the distinctive customs, language and identity of the hill people will be lost forever — to Thailand.

Nicholas Tapp

SELECT BIBLIOGRAPHY

Hinton, P., *Tribesmen and Peasants in North Thailand*, Tribal

Research Centre, Chiengmai, 1969
Kearney, R.N., *Politics and Modernisation in South and South East Asia*, Schenkman, Cambridge, Mass., 1975
Lebar, F.M., *Ethnic Groups of Mainland South East Asia*, Human Relations Area Files, New Haven, 1964
Wolf, E., Jorgensen, J., *Anthropology on the Warpath in Thailand*, New York Review of Books, November 1970
Young, G., *The Hill Tribes of Northern Thailand*, The Siam Society of Bangkok, 1974

24   India's Christians

According to the 1971 census, 2.44% of the Indians are Christian. Most of the 14.22 million Christians are to be found in the States of Kerala (4.5 million), where they constitute one-fifth of the population; West Bengal (2.51 million); Tamil Nadu (2.37 million); and Andhra Pradesh (1.82 million). There is a concentration of Christians in such small States and Union Territories as Nagaland, Mizoram and Goa. A little over half are Roman Catholic, and the remainder Protestant. Christianity in India has a long history, and many Syrian (Nestorian) Christians of Kerala claim Apostle Thomas to be the founder of their church, while others attribute the origin of their church to the Syrian Orthodox Church of Alexandria (Egypt) in the sixth century.

The modern phase of Christianity in India began with the landing of the Portuguese in Kerala in 1499, followed by the arrival of Saint Francis Xavier in Goa in 1542. It is estimated that in the mid-sixteenth century, the number of converts to Catholicism, attracted mostly from among the outcastes and low caste Hindus, was less than 100,000. By 1850, their size had probably risen to a million, when a substantial number of Protestant missionaries, mainly of British origin, arrived in India. Their efforts to proselytize were particularly successful in the tribal belts of southern Bihar and the north-eastern zone.

The proselytizing endeavour of Christian missionaries was often accompanied by the establishment of schools and colleges mainly, but not exclusively, to educate those who had embraced Christianity, so that India today still has a large number of church-run educational institutions. In the mid-1960s, for instance, the Catholic church in India managed eighty university colleges, and 6,176 schools, with a student population of well over 1.5 million. As long as these institutions remain open to all those who seek admission, they are entitled to receive government grants-in-aid for buildings and recurring expenses.

Government policy is defined under Articles 29 and 30 of the Indian Constitution of 1950: 'No citizen shall be denied admission into any educational institution maintained by the State or receiving aid out of State funds on grounds only of religion, race, caste, language or any of them'. And, Article 30: 'All minorities, whether based on religion or language, shall have the right to establish and administer educational institutions of their own choice'. The educational institutions run by Christian churches or missions are generally well regarded, but not the Christian community as a whole. Indian society remains caste conscious, and the fact that present-day Christians were once mainly low caste or outcaste Hindus is deeply rooted in the communal psyche, although in purely legal and constitutional terms they are under no disadvantage. They are seemingly active in all walks of life. Complaints made by Christian leaders concern mainly discrimination shown against the members of their community in the selection of higher grade officers in the civil service.

The Christians are well integrated in the political life of the country, but there are no exclusively Christian political organisations. The Naga Nationalist Organisation and the United Democratic Front in Nagaland are predominantly Christian simply because the vast majority of Nagas are Christian; the Kerala Congress is another example of a predominantly Christian regional party.

Prospects for the Indian Christians vary from region to region. In such border States as Nagaland and Mizoram, the problem of social and political integration with the rest of the sub-continent is rooted more in the tribal origin of the populace than its Christian belief. In Kerala and Goa, the Christian population is too important, both numerically and culturally, to be ignored, and is able to exert an influence commensurate with its size. The emotional hold of the Catholic church there tends to shift their political leanings to the right. Elsewhere, the condition of the Christian community — which, by virtue of being an urban community, is spared the social and economic oppression that is, for example, suffered by the predominantly rural Untouchables — is likely to remain as it is today.

Dilip Hiro

SELECT BIBLIOGRAPHY

Appasamy, A.J., *The Christian Task in Independent India,* Society for Promoting Christian Knowledge, London, 1951
Brown, L., *The Indian Christians of St. Thomas,* Cambridge University Press, Cambridge, 1956
Moore, F.V., *Christians in India,* Publications Division, Ministry of Information and Broadcasting, Government of India, Delhi, 1964
Pickett, J., *Christian Mass Movements in India,* Abingdon Press, New York, 1933
Plattner, F., *Christian India,* Vanguard Press, New York, 1957
Thomas, P., *Christians and Christianity in India,* Allen & Unwin, London, 1954

25   India's Muslims

The Muslims are the largest religious minority in India. They number approximately 47 million — 10% of the total population. In Kashmir, where there is a majority of Muslims, and in the south, where Muslims are a wealthy elite, there are few problems of discrimination. But the Muslims of north India are a disadvantaged group.

The antagonism felt by the Hindu majority community towards the Muslim minority is deep-rooted. Extremist Hindus detest the Muslims as the descendants of the victorious invaders who ruled India for six hundred years until the mid-eighteenth century, although most of the Muslims are converts rather than invaders or immigrants. Islam was often adopted by those who were regarded as outcasts in Hindu society because of their association with Muslims in government employment, or because their profession was unacceptable in the Hindu caste system. There were also mass spiritual conversions in the fifteenth and sixteenth centuries. British rule created intense bitterness and distrust between the Hindu and the Muslim communities, leading eventually to the Partition of 1949 and the creation of an Islamic state of Pakistan. Only a Muslim elite of about 5 million moved to the new state, while 40 million Muslims stayed behind, now lacking effective leadership.

Since Partition, most Muslims have supported the prosecular Congress party. In return, the Congress cabinet almost always includes one Muslim. It seems that Mrs Gandhi's Emergency regime won their support, because it represented an attack on Hindu reactionaries and has proscribed one of the extremist Hindu organisations. The extremist Muslim League has support only in the South: many Muslims believe that a separatist political course would only increase their isolation.

There have been serious communal riots over the last twelve years. Statistics show a steady increase in casualties:

Date	Killed and Injured in reported riots	
Jan–Dec '63	18	141
Jan–Dec '67	774	1,546
Jan–Dec '69	4,443	22,309

It is known that such incidents have been continuing in recent years, although there are no exact figures available. Observers claim that the riots are organised attacks on the Muslim community by the Hindu communal element. The government and the police did little to control the rioting or punish those responsible.

Hindu extremists demand the 'Indianisation' of the Muslims before they can become accepted citizens of India. They have considerable support: the Jan Sangh, their political party, has steadily won more seats in elections. The Muslim minority thinks of Muslim culture as equal to Hinduism, and wishes to preserve its cultural identity. Urdu, the Muslim language of the north, has not been adopted by any State and many Indian Muslims today do not know it. The existence of a Muslim University — Aligargh — and an enlightened Ministry for Cultural Affairs protects the minority culture to a certain extent.

Legally, the Muslims are under no disadvantage. India, as a secular state, prohibits any discrimination on the grounds of religion or race. Muslim personal law is allowed to exist. The Liquat-Nehru pact (1950) was intended to protect their rights as a minority.

However, they are badly represented in most spheres. A small elite have good jobs, some Muslims have held high office and there are 30 Muslims in the Lok Sabha. In the public sector, the number of Muslims is low and steadily decreasing. In the private sector, Muslims face serious discrimination. Most firms are run by Hindus, who will not employ Muslims when there are Hindu relatives and friends available. Furthermore, the Muslim educational standard is low and the competition for jobs high. The stagnating economy and high level of unemployment makes their predicament particularly serious.

The problem of the Muslim minority lies not so much in the fact of discrimination, but in the feeling of the community that they are discriminated against. Muslims think of themselves as second-rate citizens and do not bother to apply for the better jobs. Some Muslims are now demanding a quota system to ensure jobs and university places. It is unlikely that an Indian government would ever introduce such a scheme, particularly since many moderate Hindus believe Muslim grievances merely stem fron an imaginary persecution complex. It is predicted that Muslims will in the future try to resolve their problems with the help of the one major non-Hindu party — the Indian communists.

Beverley Lang

SELECT BIBLIOGRAPHY

Baig, M.R.A., *The Muslim Dilemma in India*, Vikas, Delhi, 1974
Brass, P.R., *Language, Religion and Politics in North India*, Cambridge University Press, London, 1975
Murjeeb, M., *The Indian Muslims*, Allen and Unwin, London, 1967
Smith, W.C., *Modern Islam in India*, London, 1946

Smith, D.E., *India as a Secular State,* Princeton University Press, New Jersey, 1963

26 Indonesia's Newest Minority: The East Timorese

The island of Timor has been largely bypassed by the cultural worlds of Buddhism, Hinduism and Islam which so deeply influenced the other islands of the Indonesian archipelago. Its 1,550,000 inhabitants are a complex mixture of Melanesian, Australoid, Negrito and Proto-Malay, together with a considerable influx of more recent immigrants which include Chinese, Arabs, Indians, Africans and Europeans.

Although the 700,000 West Timorese inhabitants of the Indonesian province of East Nusa Tengarra, have suffered systematic discrimination in education, government employment, and religious discrimination (most are Christians, unlike the majority of Indonesians); it is the 650,000 East Timorese who have suffered most from Indonesian authority over the past two years.

Although both halves of Timor are now almost equally poverty stricken, the island was once regarded as a rich prize for Portuguese and Dutch colonial traders who fought each other fiercely for access to the sandalwood which was an entrée into the lucrative China trade; the present boundaries between East and West Timor were settled in 1904 with the Luso-Hollandesa treaty between Portugal and Holland when most of the sandalwood was gone. Following the successful independence struggle against Dutch colonial rule, Western Timor became part of the new Republic of Indonesia in 1949, but despite the nationalism and anti-colonialism of the new Republic there was no attempt by its leaders to dislodge the Portuguese colonialists from East Timor, or from the tiny enclave of Oe-Cusse situated in West Timor. The people of East Timor continued under colonial rule from Portugal, which became more oppressive under Salazar's dictatorship. The two halves of the island developed along totally different lines, the people spoke different languages and the economies of the two halves of Timor were integrated into two different systems, in which each was a peripheral backwater.

When the Lisbon coup came in April 1974 and the Portuguese secret police were disbanded, the East Timorese aspired to self-government at last. Encouraged by the Portuguese, there was over the next two years a great deal of political discussion, experimentation and innovation in the field of political education. The people of East Timor were much freer than any of their neighbours in Indonesia to organise politically, to join or form parties and to vote in local elections during this time. In one election, organised by the Portuguese Armed Forces Movement, 90% of the candidates elected were members of Fretilin, the party which advocated independence for East Timor. Fretilin formed a coalition in January 1975 with the UDT (Timorese Democratic Union), which at first advocated remaining with Portugal but later also supported independence. Together they were recognised by local administrators as having the support of nearly 90% of the adult population, the third party, Apodeti, having the support only of its founders and their families. During 1975 the Portuguese Administration, led by the Armed Forces Movement, was trying to form a transitional government which would reflect the aspirations of the Timorese people pending a referendum on independence or integration with Indonesia, free from any outside coercion. But the Indonesian Government had other plans. As early as September 1974 President Suharto of Indonesia and Prime Minister Gough Whitlam of Australia had both agreed that 'an independent East Timor would be an unviable state and a potential threat to the area', and tacitly agreed it should be integrated with Indonesia. Despite an outcry of public opinion against this point of view both in Australia and in East Timor itself, events have shown that the Indonesian plan to integrate East Timor, 'Operation Komodo', was launched in the belief that it would not be opposed by the Australian government.

Briefly, 'Operation Komodo' relied initially on simple propaganda, then attempts to subvert Timorese party leaders, finally resorting to military invasion when these failed. From April 1975 leaders of all three parties were invited to Jakarta and attempts made to buy them off; this was hardly necessary with the Apodeti leaders, but while it succeeded somewhat with the UDT, it failed totally with Fretilin. In August the UDT leadership, believing that Indonesia would step in on their side, attempted a coup which failed but which triggered off a civil war lasting about six weeks. The UDT and Apodeti leaders, were forced across the border into Indonesian Timor by the victorious Fretilin forces. The Portuguese administration removed itself to a small offshore island and Fretilin was left to form an administration although it still recognised Portuguese sovereignty.

Across the border in West Timor the anti-Fretilin parties accepted Indonesian military assistance in return for announcing their support for integration. In September 1975 the first limited attacks were launched across the border and while Australian Intelligence had evidence of Indonesian troops inside East Timor, the Australian Government denied any invasion was taking place, and subsequently covered up the deaths of two Australian TV news teams shot under orders from the Indonesian military near the border. Only hours after President Ford and Henry Kissinger had left Jakarta, a full scale invasion was launched in the early hours of 7 December. Eyewitnesses of the first few hours of the invasion reported widespread indiscriminate killing, including a group of Chinese who came to welcome the Indonesians. Most Timorese retreated to the mountains with Fretilin and have been able to resist for some time.

Several days after the invasion the UN General Assembly adopted resolution 3485 (XXX) in which Indonesia was called on 'to withdraw without delay its forces from the territory in order to enable the people of the territory freely to exercise their right to self determination and independence'. The Security Council unanimously adopted a similar resolution in December and again in April 1976. Indonesia however, has totally disregarded these resolutions and actually increased the number of troops in East Timor as resistance from the Timorese people continued.

The Government of Indonesia also put a blockade of warships around the whole island preventing foreign journalists, medical teams, or other independent observers from visiting East Timor, in marked contrast to the period of administration by Fretilin. The International Red Cross has been excluded from the territory.

On 31 May 1976, the Indonesian Government staged an 'act of self-determination' in Dili, the capital of East Timor, but the United Nations and many countries including Australia, the U.S.A., Portugal and Japan all refused invitations to be present or to recognise it as such. The Indonesian Government declared

East Timor to be the 27th province of Indonesia on 17 July. In so doing it incurred the criticism of many members of the Conference of Non-Aligned nations held in Colombo, in August 1976, when several speeches were made against the annexation, and East Timor was added to the list of non-self governing territories 'still to be liberated' — the first time support has been given by that body to a people fighting one of its own members.

Early in 1976 one of the UDT leaders claimed that 50–60,000 had been killed since August 1975; if this is so it represents nearly one-tenth of the population of East Timor and must include many women and children.

The administration installed by the Indonesian Government is hardly democratic; it is headed by Arnaldo Araujo, who has long been unpopular in various quarters in East Timor. At the local level the Indonesians have brought back many of the old dictatorial chiefs used by the Portuguese who had been removed under the Armed Forces Movement's democratising prog- ramme. In the mountains, which cover a large part of East Timor, the Fretilin leadership, still largely intact, is broadcasting messages to the outside world via Darwin weekly, and internal radio broadcasts can also be monitored in northern Australia. They broadcast in East Timorese languages but have recently added Indonesian which suggests that Timorese from the Indonesian side of the border have also recently joined Fretilin.

Indonesia feared an independent East Timor partly for the example it would set to other islands in the Indonesian archipelago; it characterised Fretilin as 'Communist' at a time when Fretilin wanted an independence guaranteed by Indonesia and Australia. But the invasion has not served the interests of the Indonesian Government as it has unleashed criticism from within and outside Indonesia, that may have long term effects on its structure.

Helen Hill

Select Bibliography

Dunn, J.S., *The Timor Story,* Parliament of Australia, Legislative Research Service, Canberra, July 1976
Freney, D., *Timor: Freedom Caught Between the Powers,* Spokesman Books, Nottingham, 1975
Hicks, D., 'An Introduction to Timorese Ethnography', in Frank

Lebar (ed), *Ethnic Groups of Insular South East Asia,* Human Relations Area Files, New Haven, 1972

Hill, H., *The Timor Story,* Timor Information Service, Melbourne, January 1976

Hoadley, J.S., *The Future of Portuguese Timor,* Occasional Paper No. 27 Institute of South East Asian Studies, Singapore, March 1976

Ormeling, F.J., *The Timor Problem — A Geographical Interpretation of an Underdeveloped Island,* Nijhoff, The Hague, 1956

Timor Task Force, *Report on a Visit to East Timor,* Australian Council for Overseas Aid, October 1975

27   The Inuit: Eskimos of North America

The Eskimos are the most widely scattered aboriginal people, living in small settlements along the coastlines of Greenland (40,000, largely mixed European-Eskimo stock), Labrador, Newfoundland, Quebec and the totally Arctic North-West territories of Canada (17,000), Alaska (30,000) and Siberia. They also live in the harshest conditions in the world, with which their nomadic life — hunting and, to a lesser extent, fishing, in small close kinship groups — established an equilibrium over 4–5,000 years before the first contacts with Russian and European culture. The caribou and sea mammals (seals, narwhales etc), formed the basis of a self-sufficient and, of necessity, a wasteless economy, but after initial exploration-contact from the seventeenth century onwards Europeans started trapping for the Arctic fox in particular for trade in Southern markets. This introduced the Eskimos, both to the breaking of their own taboos on trapping, and to an early consumer economy. It also introduced European diseases, like small-pox, measles and influenza, which killed great numbers, and which still affect outlying communities badly, although the population loss has been made up. Competition for food sources, particularly the whales, also committed the Eskimos to dietary changes which had a deleterious effect. Eskimo language, based on composite noun formations incorporating attributes and virtues, represented the compact inter-relationship of roles and values within traditional Eskimo society. The word Inuit, by which the Eskimos prefer to be known, means 'human beings'.

Although most Eskimos now live in settlements where trading posts — particularly those of the Hudson Bay Company — and mission stations were based, a few are still nomadic. Neither the early traders, nor the determinedly de-heathenising missionaries (the Bible was translated in 1908) were particularly sensitive to the strength or subtleties of Eskimo culture, and brought with them the law to enforce the submission that their own sense of superiority required of these people. But the informal pressures to settle during the past fifty years came from an increasing dependency on medical help, a weak cash economy — requiring welfare subvention — administered by whites, responsible to Ottawa or the U.S. Bureau of Indian Affairs, or Copenhagen, to whom nomadism is bureaucratically irksome. (Little is known about the Eskimos in Siberia, but their population seems stable, and economy still self-sufficient.) The Eskimos became an administered people, peripheral, demoralised by the breakdown of their society and ambivalent towards the attractions of the northward encroachment of white society, in which they were, and are, not allowed to participate fully. Life-expectancy remains in the 20's, compared with the 30's for Indians and 60's for whites. Statistics show that 25% of school age children were not enrolled: apart from remoteness, Eskimo parents are increasingly concerned at the unsuitability of much of the content of education, giving inadequate emphasis to Eskimo culture, insufficient examination of the problems they encounter in the modern world, and especially the negative image of their culture propagated in text-books and by their teachers. Most Eskimos live in one-room rental houses, without running water, or shacks and tents, while white Canadian housing in the Arctic is built to southern urban standards, with salaries commensurate to pay for them.

A relatively small number of Eskimo men are involved in the resource exploration and exploitation that started in Alaska and Canada in the 1960s. Mineral stake-outs, oil and natural gas production are changing the vast areas of the Arctic more rapidly than 400 years of contact, and have become the gravest threat to Eskimo culture and well-being yet faced. The influx of white Canadians, particularly to the rich McKenzie River area, both absorbs the available food resources and prevents the Eskimo from either continuing to exploit his own usufructuary hunting territories, or to become self-sufficient wage-earners. The State of Alaska passed the Alaska Native Claims Settlement Act 1971, which gave the Eskimos (with the Indians and Aleuts) rights and title to about 40 million acres, while the Canadian government established a Land Claims project, to decide which lands the Eskimos may get in perpetuity, the compensation for areas that have been, or will be, taken up, and the mechanism by which the Eskimos may be involved in their own administration. Indians and Eskimos called for a halt on exploration and development of the resources pending the settlement of land claims, and the essential problem of enforcing a comprehensive northern land use policy (including the payment of royalties to the Eskimoes; and prevention of environmental damage), but the Canadian government — and the pressures of the U.S. 'energy' crises, allowed the operating companies to continue. The former Minister for Indian Affairs and Northern Development, Jean Chretien, declared that 'the potential of the north is limitless . . . the decision is made. It has been made by the whites, government and companies . . . the resources will serve the interests of Canadian capitalist society — the interests of the Inuit are of secondary importance'.

There is some growing political organisation among the Eskimos to achieve land rights, amid the uncertainties which have added to the historically confused objectives of all solutions to the 'Eskimo problem'. There is little emigration, but an increasing gap between the generations under these accelerated pressures. Individual Eskimos are in no position to oppose the government, or match the adventurers, who have little concern for them and are by no means figures of the past. The non-viability of the Indian reserve system, with its built-in dependence and thence amenability, should not be perpetuated in an Eskimo enclave that is not sustainable with a mixed economy; nor will mere cash payments, as given under the James Bay scheme, solve the problem of where or how Eskimos should live in a white dominated society. Optimistic Government statements about increased freedom of opportunity to Eskimos, do not take into account both what has been lost to the Eskimo livelihood, nor the very real problem of prejudice and confusion of cultural values.

C.W./G.A.

SELECT BIBLIOGRAPHY

Brody, H., *The People's Land — Eskimos and Whites in the Eastern Arctic,* Penguin, Harmondsworth, 1975
Frenchen, P., *Boom of the Eskimos,* Arthur Barker, London, 1962
Gubber, N., *The Nunamuit Eskimos: Hunters of Caribou,* Yale University Press, 1965
Inuit Monthly, Ottawa, Ontario
Jenners, D., *Eskimo Administration: Canada,* Arctic Institute of North America Technical Paper No. 14, May 1964
Eskimo Administration: Greenland Arctic Institute of North America, Technical Paper No. 19

28   The Kashmiri

The state of Jammu and Kashmir covers an area of 84,471 square miles in the northwest corner of the subcontinent. It consists of three distinct regions: the Vale of Kashmir, which contains half of the state's population and is 93% Muslim; Jammu, which contains a slight Hindu majority; and a diverse group of frontier areas, among them Ladakh, a sparsely populated region with close cultural and linguistic ties to Tibet. These regions are often referred to collectively as Kashmir. The total population of the state is roughly 6,000,000 of whom about 77% are Muslim and 20% are Hindu; the balance are Buddhist and Sikh.

Historical Background: In the 14th century Muslim invaders conquered the Vale of Kashmir, bringing to an end centuries of Buddhist and Hindu rule. In 1587 the Vale was absorbed into the Moghul Empire, and in 1752 it passed to the Afghans who ruled until 1819 when they were displaced by the Sikhs. By the end of this five century era of Muslim rule most of the population had converted to Islam.

The modern state of Jammu and Kashmir came into being in 1846 when the British defeated the Sikhs in the First Sikh War. Rather than annex the Vale directly, the British turned over rule of the territory to the Hindu maharaja of Jammu in exchange for

7½ million rupees. They thus gained the security of a buffer state between their Indian empire and Russia and China without assuming the expense and responsibility of administering the state. In so doing, however, they planted the seeds of future conflict by installing a Hindu ruler over a largely Muslim population.

The Hindu dynasty ruled Kashmir for a century. During this period the Muslim majority suffered neglect, was excluded from the civil service and the military, and lived under orthodox Hindu law. In the 1930's — stimulated by the example of Gandhi's movement in India — Kashmiris began to agitate against Hindu rule, and by the eve of British withdrawal from the subcontinent two popular movements were afoot. United in their opposition to the maharaja, these movements were divided against one another. One, led by Sheikh Mohammed Abdullah, was secular in outlook and favored independence for Kashmir; the other was communal in outlook and favoured inclusion of Kashmir in the incipient Islamic state of Pakistan.

Under the terms agreed upon for the partition of the subcontinent in 1947, the rulers of princely states, such as Kashmir, were given the choice of acceding either to India or Pakistan. In view of its location and communal composition, Kashmir was generally expected to accede to Pakistan. But the Hindu maharaja of the predominantly Muslim state delayed his decision, apparently in an effort to retain his throne by creating a stalemate between India and Pakistan. This strategy provoked a local revolt against his rule and an invasion of Pathan tribesmen from Pakistan. Under the pressure of these events, the maharaja acceded to India. India accepted the accession on a provisional basis, declaring that once order had been restored, it would hold a plebiscite to ascertain the will of the people. India then sent troops into Kashmir to repel the tribal invasion. Pakistan, which had openly supported the rebels and their Pathan allies, committed regular troops several months later. War between the two newborn nations continued until the end of 1948 when a U.N.-supervised ceasefire was established. The ceasefire line divided Kashmir, leaving Pakistan in control of the thinly populated northern third of the state and India in control of the bulk of the state, including the Vale of Kashmir.

During and after the 1947–48 conflict the Indian pledge to hold a plebiscite was embodied in a series of U.N. Security

Council resolutions. Although both India and Pakistan accepted the principle of self-determination for Kashmir, each set conditions unacceptable to the other. India argued that Pakistan had been guilty of aggression and conditioned the holding of a plebiscite on the withdrawal of Pakistani forces from Kashmir. Pakistan stressed the geographic, cultural, and economic contiguity of Kashmir to Pakistan and called for a universal plebiscite to be held after an impartial Kashmir government had been established. Despite repeated U.N. efforts, the dispute has remained stalemated and a plebiscite has never been held.

Sheikh Abdullah, who had led the nationalist movement prior to partition, became prime minister of Kashmir in 1948. While Abdullah preferred accession to India over accession to Pakistan, he was dedicated above all to the cause of Kashmiri independence. He insisted that the Indian Constitution was inapplicable to the special case of Kashmir and declared that the state was autonomous in all respects except foreign affairs, defence, and communications. After negotiations between Abdullah and Pandit Nehru, India formally acknowledged the special status of Kashmir in Article 370 of its Constitution. But in 1953 Abdullah was deposed by a faction within his party which favoured closer ties with India.

Over the next twenty years — most of which Abdullah spent in prison or detention — Kashmir was gradually integrated into India. During this period the Kashmiris were denied not only a plebiscite, but also free and open state elections. Advocates of self-determination were vigorously suppressed and state elections were held virtually without opposition. Thus, the actions of the pro-India state assembly, which in 1956 ratified the accession and in 1957 proclaimed Kashmir an integral part of India, can hardly be said to have expressed the popular will.

Denied expression through the ballot, popular sentiment found other outlets during the mid–1960's. The precipitating event was the theft of a holy relic — a hair of the Prophet — from a mosque in Srinagar. It was feared that this incident would lead to violence between Muslims and Hindus, and it did in fact spark serious rioting in Bengal. But, despite considerable communal tension, such fears were not realized in Kashmir. Rather, the incident triggered an outpouring of resentment against the state administration and, by extension, against India. The hair was recovered after two weeks, but the agitation continued. In an effort to deflate the protest movement, the government released Abdullah, but within a matter of months he was under arrest again. This provoked a new wave of protests in which followers of Abdullah were joined by groups favouring accession to Pakistan. A non-violent campaign of civil disobedience was launched and there was some anti-Indian guerrilla activity.

Events within Kashmir exacerbated tensions between India and Pakistan. Pakistan condemned the Indian policy of assimilating Kashmir; India countered by charging that Pakistan had sent infiltrators into the state to stir up unrest. Border clashes soon escalated into the second Indo-Pakistani war over Kashmir. A ceasefire was achieved in the fall of 1965, and in 1966 the two nations withdrew to the 1949 ceasefire line.

In the aftermath of the war, the self-determination movement assumed a more militant cast, as Muslim students, disillusioned with the efforts of their more moderate elders, intensified their protests. India responded with a harsh crackdown. Invoking the Defence of India Rules — first instituted during the Sino-Indian war in 1962 and later to be used as the vehicle for Mrs. Gandhi's suspension of civil rights in 1975 — the government imposed strict censorship, jailed virtually all advocates of self-determination, and promulgated measures designed to retard the development of opposition, such as a regulation prohibiting gatherings of more than five people without prior permission.

Such draconian measures were somewhat relaxed later in the 1960's and India endeavoured to make its control of Kashmir more palatable to the population by investing heavily in the state's economic development. But the events of 1965 — and the heavy Indian military presence in the state — made it clear that India would not tolerate resistance to its integration of Kashmir. The adaptation of Kashmiris to this circumstance has been exemplified by recent turns in the career of Sheikh Abdullah, who was for so long the most articulate voice — and the symbol — of Kashmiri aspirations for self-determination. Abdullah emerged from his most recent period of detention in 1972. Over the next two years he and Mrs. Gandhi negotiated an agreement under which he became chief minister of the state in February, 1975. Upon resuming leadership of the state, after a lapse of 22 years, Abdullah declared that the merger of Kashmir with India was 'final and irrevocable.'

Although the basic issue remains unresolved, the Indo-

Pakistani dispute over Kashmir appears less volatile today than at any time since Independence. This is less a reflection of reasoned reconciliation between the two nations than of a shift in the balance of power on the subcontinent since the 1971 Indo-Pakistani war over Bangladesh. Weakened by defeat and dismemberment, Pakistan is simply in no position to challenge Indian control of Kashmir by force.

It is likely that the ceasefire line will eventually be converted into a formal boundary. Such a partition of the state would benefit the Kashmiris by relieving the uncertainty which has clouded their future and by minimizing the likelihood that Kashmir will once again become a battlefield. But unless the Kashmiris themselves are allowed to participate in fashioning such a resolution, their fate will once again have been set by others. And their basic grievance — denial of the right of self-determination — will remain.

Since the suspension of civil rights throughout India in June, 1975, it has been difficult to discern the intensity of self-determination sentiment in Kashmir. It is possible that India's reinstatement of Abdullah and its substantial investments in the state's economic development have won it the allegiance of the Kashmiris. But the present appearance of calm may be deceptive. A large demonstration of orthodox Muslims and pro-Pakistani students in June, 1976 suggests that a substantial portion of the population remains unreconciled to Indian rule. It seems likely, however, that the present suspension of civil rights will inhibit the resurgence of opposition. Thus, the prospects of the self-determination issue being resolved — or even aired — now hinge on the overall Indian political situation.

Jamie Kalven

SELECT BIBLIOGRAPHY

Brecher, M., *The Struggle for Kashmir,* Oxford, 1953
Dixon, O., *Report to the Security Council,* U.N. Security Council, 15 September 1950
Korbe, J., *Danger in Kashmir,* Princeton, 1954
Lamb, A., *The Kashmir Problem: A Historical Survey,* Praeger, 1966
Lockwood, D. *Sheikh Abdullah and the Politics of Kashmir,* Asian Survey, May 1969

Lockwood, D., *Kashmir: Sheikh Abdullah's Reinstatement,* The World Today, June 1975
Mohammed Abdullah, Sheikh, *Kashmir, India and Pakistan,* Foreign Affairs, April 1965

29   The Latvians

The Latvians are a Baltic people, living on the shores of the Gulf of Riga and in the river valleys of the Daugava and Gauja. They speak an Indo-European language, closely related to Lithuanian and the now-extinct Old Prussian. Since the 13th century they have been colonised by foreign powers — Germans, Russians and Swedes — and only in the 20th century did they achieve a short period of independence.

In the 13th century, the pagan Latvian tribes were first colonised by the German Order of knight-monks, the Brethren of the Sword, and later by a second German order, the Teutonic Knights. The German knightly orders established two provinces, Livonia and Courland, which continued as political entities until the 16th century. The Latvians were forcibly converted to Catholicism and became serfs, with the German knights as their feudal landlords. In 1561, Livonia became a province of the Kingdom of Lithuania-Poland for a time, while Courland became an independent duchy with a German dynasty. In 1622, Livonia became a Swedish colony, but in 1721 it came under Russian rule, as a result of the Great Northern War. In 1795, with the third and last partition of Poland, Courland too became part of the Russian Empire. The most eastern region of Latvia, Latgale, remained part of Lithuania-Poland until the 18th century when it was also absorbed into the Russian Empire.

Under the Russian Tsarist Empire, the Latvians were subjected to a double colonization. The central government was Russian, and in the later 19th century Russian was the language of official instruction in schools, but most of the local landlords and officials were Germans — the so-called 'Baltic barons'. In the 19th century, a national cultural revival movement led to the

establishment of Latvian as a literary language and the growth of
a nationalist political movement. The 1905 anti-Tsarist
Revolution was particularly violent in the Latvian provinces,
where the Russian army was attacked and hundreds of
farmhouses belonging to German landlords were burned down.
As a result of the 1905 disturbances, the Latvian language was
allowed in schools for the first time as a medium of instruction. In
1914, the First World War broke out; by 1915 the German Army
had reached the River Daugava. Latvian national regiments were
formed within the Tsarist Army and successfully held the front
until 1917. After the February Revolution of 1917, a struggle for
power between various political factions began, not only in the
Russian Empire as a whole, but in Latvia. Certain Latvian army
regiments had an important role in the establishment of
Bolshevik power after the October Revolution, and after a later
short-lived attempt to establish a Soviet Republic of Latvia in
1918–19, a number of Latvian Communists left Latvia and went
to live in the Soviet Union. In Latvia, there was a confused period
of fighting in 1917–19, as there were at least four different
military forces in the area — Bolshevik, White Russian, German
and Latvian nationalist units under the Latvian National Council.
This Council was composed of non-Bolshevik parties and
proclaimed an independent republic of Latvia on 18 November
1918, although they only established stable rule over Latvia as a
whole in July, 1919.

The National Council was headed by K. Ulmanis, the leader of
the Peasant League, who later became Prime Minister after
elections held in 1920. The Peasant League remained in power
until 1940: it was a party which drew its strength from the
re-distribution of land it organized in the 1920's. The huge
estates which formerly belonged to German and Russian
landlords were re-distributed among the Latvian peasants who
had a claim to the land. This policy made Latvia a land of small
farmers, who gave their support almost entirely to the Peasant
League, although there was an influential Social-Democratic
Party, which drew its support largely from the urban areas.

In June 1940 under the terms of the German-Soviet pact
between Hitler and Stalin, Latvia was occupied by the Red Army
and a Communist government was set up. In July 1940,
Soviet-style 'elections' were held: only Communist Party
candidates were allowed and the principle of electoral secrecy was

openly contravened. As a result, 97.6% of the electorate 'voted' for the Communist Party. Shortly afterwards the new government applied to join the U.S.S.R. as a Soviet Socialist Republic; Latvia was incorporated into the Soviet Union in August 1940.

The Soviet take-over included annexation of one of the eastern districts of Latvia — the Pytalovo area in eastern Latvia. It was followed by mass arrests and deportations of social groups thought to be hostile to the new Soviet government: small farmers and their families, army officers, civil servants, clergymen and so on. In 1940–41 34,205 Latvians were deported to remote areas of Siberia and the Far East.

During the ensuing period of German occupation following Hitler's invasion of the U.S.S.R. in June, 1941, thousands of Latvians were taken to Germany as labourers. Also 10–12,000 Latvians and 56,000 Latvian Jews lost their lives in German concentration camps. About 115,000 Latvians left the country in 1944–45, mostly for refugee camps in Germany: having experienced the earlier period of Soviet rule, they preferred not to await the return of the Soviet Army to Latvia. The re-establishment of a Soviet government was followed by two large-scale deportations of Latvian social groups considered undesirable by the Soviet authorities: in 1945, about 40,000 people were deported, largely from the Courland area; and in 1949, about 60,000 people were deported — most of the latter were small farmers who had resisted collectivization. The majority of these people were transported to labour camps in remote areas of the Soviet Union. Apart from these two mass deportations, another 15,000 Latvians were sent to Soviet labour camps outside Latvia in the years 1945–56. Some of those who survived were able to return to Latvia in the 1960's, but some are still denied a residence permit in their homeland.

Meanwhile, there has been a huge influx of Russian immigrants into Latvia. In 1935, there were 206,000 Russians in Latvia, out of a population of just under two million while in 1970, there were 705,000 Russians, 29.8% of the population of the Latvian SSR. If Belorussians and Ukrainians are added, this percentage rises to 36.1%. According to the 1970 census, out of a total population of 2,364,000 only 1,342,000 (56.8%) are Latvians. The Latvian birth rate is lower than that of the immigrant Russian population: the annual increase in population since 1959 has been 24,600, but of these *only 4,000 are Latvians.* Russian workers are attracted to Latvia by the better housing and higher living standards available there. The majority of Russian immigrants (79.6%) settle in the cities, as living standards are lower in the countryside.

It is significant that the relative numbers of Latvians and Russians in the Latvian Communist Party are not published and are, therefore, difficult to calculate. However, the figures of total Latvian membership in the Soviet Communist Party (1973) lead to the conclusion that Latvians could not constitute more than 43% of the Communist Party of their own republic, and that this percentage could be as low as 33%. Russian membership of the Latvian Communist Party is calculated to be about 40%, while Latvian Communist Party members are only about 3.4% of the Latvian population as a whole. Only 47% of Communist Party officials in Latvia are Latvians, according to a letter written by 17 Latvian Communists in 1972. Out of 117 Party regional secretaries, 47 are Russians. In Riga, the capital city of Latvia, only 18% of Communist Party members are Latvians, while the actual percentage of Latvians in Riga is 40%. Latvians are discriminated against in certain government ministries: for example, out of 1,500 employees of the Ministry of the Interior in Riga, only 300 are Latvians. A large proportion of the Party and government leadership in Latvia are either Russians or Ukrainians who do not speak Latvian (for example, Belukha, Second Secretary of the Communist Party, and Bondaletov, Deputy Chairman of the Council of Ministers) or Latvian Communists who were brought up in Russia after 1918 and often speak Latvian very badly (for example, G. Rubenis, Chairman of the Council of Ministers, and Petersons, the Party Secretary for Industrial Affairs). The Latvian Communist Party Central Committee, the real nucleus of power in the republic, has 11 members. Of these, 4 are Russians who speak no Latvian at all, 6 are Russian-born Latvians (4 of whom speak the language badly), while only one member, P. Strautmanis, is a true Latvian who is fluent in the Latvian language. Meetings of the Central Committee and the Council of Ministers take place in the Russian language.

In 1959–60, about 9,000 Latvian Communists were purged from the Party, because of their 'nationalist Communist' views. These were headed by E. Berklavs, then Deputy Chairman of the

Latvian SSR Council of Ministers, and I. Pinskis, head of the Latvian Trade Union organization, who had been calling for a curb on the number of immigrants from the other Soviet republics, conservation of most of the Latvian republic's production for consumption by its own citizens, and a policy in education aimed at teaching Latvian to Russian immigrants rather than introducing bi-lingualism in Russian for Latvian children. These views were criticized as approximating to 'bourgeois nationalism'.

Paralleling this increase in the number of Russians resident in Latvia since the war, there has been a widespread Russification of communications and 'internationalization' of social institutions. This is especially true of Riga, the capital city, where Latvians are in a minority. Russians make little effort to learn the native language (only 15.6% of Russians living in Latvia speak Latvian) and expect any meetings or gatherings in which they participate to be held in Russian. Latvians are expected to know Russian and many jobs require a fluent knowledge of Russian. In fact, 45.3% of Latvians are fluent speakers of Russian.

There is an avowed 'bi-lingual' policy in Latvian schools from the kindergarten upwards. This is not a true bi-lingualism, as it is designed only to make Latvian children bi-lingual in Russian, not Russian children bi-lingual in Latvian. In Russian-language schools, Latvian is a minority subject, while in Latvian-language schools, Russian is not only a compulsory subject, but is often the medium in which other subjects are regularly taught. Pioneer meetings for children are mostly conducted in Russian, as are teachers' meetings.

53% of books and 52% of journals published in the Latvian SSR are in the Latvian language — *only just over half.* Russian classics are reprinted, but rarely Latvian pre-Soviet writers. One channel on radio and television is in Russian, while a third of the programmes on the other channel are also in Russian. National festivals which Latvians have celebrated for centuries, such as the Midsummer 'Ligo' Festival, were officially banned for many years, but recently, since 1970, they have merely been ignored by the authorities. At national song festivals Russian songs have been introduced into the programme. Latvian theatres, choirs and orchestras are made to understand that they must include Russian plays and songs in their repertoire, while Russian companies in Latvia are under no obligation to include Latvian plays or songs in their productions. The capital city, Riga, now has 6 administrative regions, 4 of which have Russian names. Streets in Riga are named after all kinds of Russian writers, politicians and generals, while streets originally named after the great Latvian writers Krisjans Valdemars and Aspazija have been given new Russian names.

21% of families in the Latvian SSR are now mixed — with one Russian and one Latvian parent. 35.5% of marriages are mixed. However, almost 60% of teenagers from mixed families chose Latvian as their native language, according to a survey published in the U.S.S.R. in the 1960's.

In recent years, Latvians — both nationalist and Communist — have been making their views on Russification known. There have been silent demonstrations at the grave of I. Cakste, the first president of the Latvian independent republic, with people leaving wreaths of flowers in the national colours — dark red and white. Similar wreaths are regularly left at the unmarked graves of victims of the Soviet 1940 invasion, at the National Cemetery, and at the Freedom Monument in the centre of Riga, especially on 18 November which is Latvian Independence Day. Some people have been arrested for this.

In 1972, a group of 17 Latvian Communists wrote a letter to West European Communist parties, describing most of the Russification measures outlined above, and appealing for help in resisting this 'brotherly internationalism' and in preserving national character. They appealed also on behalf of Soviet Jews and other minorities who had even less opportunity for national self-expression than the Latvians. They emphasised that they were not against socialism, but against its distortion into Russian chauvinism. They felt that such a distortion was actually harmful to the image of socialism.

Latvia is perhaps the most affected by Russian encroachment out of the three Baltic republics. Its population has presented the least resistance to assimilation. This is largely due to political economic factors. Latvia was the most industrialized of the three republics, and had the lowest native birth rate. The immigration of Russian workers to the industrial regions was thus made easier. There is also more of a feeling of political impotence among the Latvian intelligentsia than among the Lithuanians, who are united by religion as well as nationality, or the Estonians, who have a much higher national morale. This may be due partly to the 1959–62 purge of the Latvian Communist Party and the loss of national hopes this implied. The large-scale Russian immigration into urban areas also makes it more difficult for the local population to preserve its ethnic values.

In recent years there has been a tendency for Latvian national activists to unite with other fighters for human rights in the U.S.S.R. as a whole. For example, in June 1975, a statement from representatives of the Latvian and Estonian democrats called for a true implementation of human rights throughout the country.

Marite Sapiets

SELECT BIBLIOGRAPHY

American Latvian Association, *Latvija Sodien,* Washington DC, 1972
Katz et al, *Handbook of Major Soviet Nationalities,* New York, 1975
Latvijas PSR Tautas Saimnicieba 1973 Gada, Moscow, 1974
Mezgailis, B., Zvidrins, P., *Padomju Latvijas Iedzivotaji,* Riga, 1973
Determination of their Nationality by Teenagers in Nationally-Mixed Families, Sovetskaya Etnografiya, No. 3, 1968
Rauch, G. von, *The Baltic States — The Years of Independence 1917–40,* University of California, 1974
Rutkis, J., *Latvia, Country and People,* Stockholm, 1967
Spekke, A., *History of Latvia,* Stockholm, 1975
Widmer, M.J., *Nationalism and Communism in Latvia,* unpublished dissertation, Harvard, 1969

30   Lithuanians in The U.S.S.R.

There are about 2,800,000 Lithuanians in the U.S.S.R. (1962); all except 200,000 live in the territory of the Lithuanian Soviet Socialist Republic. The Lithuanians are a non-Slav people; their language belongs to the Baltic Indo-European group.

At one time, in the 16th and 17th centuries, Lithuania was a powerful state, united in a double-kingdom with Poland, and during this period the Lithuanians came to share the strong popular allegiance to the Catholic Church prevalent in Poland. From 1795 to 1917, Lithuania was part of the Russian Empire, ruled by the Tsars from Moscow, subjected to a campaign of Russification in education and public life; at one time, even books in the Lithuanian language were forbidden. This history of Russian repression in Lithuania must be borne in mind in analysing the feelings of modern Lithuanians towards the Soviet regime: the present is constantly compared with the Tsarist-period in present-day illegal Lithuanian publications.

From 1918 to 1940 Lithuania was an independent state, like the other Baltic States, Latvia and Estonia. This was a period of industrial and agricultural prosperity and saw a great flowering of national education and culture. In June 1940, Lithuania was invaded by 300,000 Soviet troops and forcibly incorporated into the U.S.S.R., after an 'election' in which the usual 99% were said to have voted for Communist party candidates. About 35,000 possible opponents of the new regime, together with their wives and children, were deported to labour camps and exile in Soviet Asia. This process was interrupted by the German invasion of the Soviet Union. Unlike some other national groups in the Soviet Union, the Lithuanians avoided collaboration with the Germans and organised anti-Nazi resistance groups, so that German rule in Lithuania 1941–44 was scarcely less harsh than Soviet rule had been. The return of the Soviet army in 1944, and the re-establishment of the Soviet regime, led to further deportations (involving 200–300/000 people) in 1944–51, and the total elimination of organised political opposition. This took longer in Lithuania than in other Baltic countries, because of the lengthy campaign by a popularly-supported partisan movement against the Soviet regime. According to Soviet figures alone, about 20,000 'bandits' were executed during the late 1940s. This movement was eventually crushed, and the Communist Party of Lithuania established complete control over every aspect of Lithuanian life and culture by the early 1950s. At this time, a great many government posts and leading jobs were held by Russians, although now the majority of such posts are filled by Lithuanians.

Although conditions have vastly improved since the death of Stalin in 1953, and about 30–40,000 of those deported have been allowed to return, the Soviet government is under no illusions as to the loyalty of its 2½ million Lithuanian citizens. They have resisted post-war Russian immigration (about 85% of the population of the Lithuanian SSR is Lithuanian, while its sister republic, Latvia, now has a non-Latvian population of 40%); only about 2% of the Lithuanian population belong to the Communist party. After the 1968 events in Czechoslovakia, a young Lithuanian, Romas Kalanta, emulated Jan Palach's protest against the Russian invasion by burning himself to death in the main square of Kaunas: this was followed by days of nationalist demonstrations in Kaunas, which had to be put down by Russian troops.

The Soviet regime concentrates on two targets: One is 'bourgeois nationalism', which is regularly denounced in the Soviet press and linked with Fascism — a wholly unfounded charge in Lithuania. (In connection with this, a young Lithuanian, M. Tamonis, was recently placed in a psychiatric hospital for refusing to renovate a monument to the Red Army until a monument to Stalin's victims was erected). The other 'anti-Soviet' manifestation in Lithuanian life which is attacked is the Catholic Church. The atheist campaign over the past 30 years, has involved the closure of hundreds of churches, the abolition of monasteries and strict limitation on the numbers of seminary students, but it is resisted strenuously for membership of the Catholic Church is identified with national identity, in much the same way as in Poland. Religious teachers are harassed, dismissed, or put on trial, while the press consistently denounces religion; yet about 80–85% of the Lithuanian population are baptised Catholics, are married and buried in Catholic churches.

The Lithuanian human rights movement, which has recently sprung up, is linked directly with Catholicism. Ever since 1972, this movement has published an underground journal — *The Chronicle of the Lithuanian Catholic Church*; 20 issues have so far appeared. The journal, which is written in Russian and Lithuanian, has obvious links with the Russian dissident movement and its *Chronicle of Current Events,* yet its much greater grass-roots support is immediately obvious, it is the source of most contemporary information about Lithuania. The *Lithuanian Chronicle* includes petitions signed by thousands of people, including about a quarter of the country's priests, and details of those people persecuted for their Catholic faith or national allegiance in schools, hospitals, universities and churches all over Lithuania. It publishes letters from ordinary workers and bishops alike and includes articles on Russification in schools and pollution of the Lithuanian countryside. Trials have been held recently in which young Lithuanians were sentenced to terms in labour camps for producing and distributing the *Chronicle.* Attempts by the Soviet authorities to have the journal denounced by the Lithuanian bishops have failed.

There is no prospect of a representative government in Lithuania, until there is a corresponding change in the Soviet system as a whole. Any revolt would be quite hopeless and would lead only to further repression. Links with the Russian dissident movement are strong and will certainly continue.

Marite Sapiets

SELECT BIBLIOGRAPHY

Beeson, T., *Discretion and Valour,* Fontana, 1974
Bociurkiw, Prof. B., *Religious Dissent in the U.S.S.R.; Lithuanian Catholics,* (unpublished paper, available from Keston College), 1974
Brizgys, V., *Religious Conditions in Lithuania under Soviet Russian Occupation,* Chicago, 1968
Chronicle of Current Events, Amnesty International
Chronicle of the Lithuanian Catholic Church, Nos. 4–11, New York
Delran, N.J., *The Violations of Human Rights in Soviet Occupied Lithuania,* 1972
Marshall, R., *Aspects of Religion in the Soviet Union,* Chicago, 1971
Vardy, Prof. S., *Lithuania under the Soviets,* New York, 1965

31   Maoris of New Zealand

The first known settlers came to New Zealand around 700 AD, being people of Polynesian stock, and settlement continued over the next six centuries. During the period 1350–1650, traditional Maori society and culture developed and consolidated from its Polynesian heritage. The Maoris' strong links with the supernatural — they always had a large family of gods — were extended into local geographical areas and features. Gods were incorporated into parts of mountain ranges or cliff faces and helped strengthen the ties of the local tribe or group with that location. Economically, the Maori was a rural agriculturalist, cultivating land as well as hunting and fishing for game.

In 1642, Abel Tasman the explorer, set foot in New Zealand and introduced the first white people, or *pakehas* to the islands. The main *pakeha* immigration occurred after Captain Cook's visit over 100 years later in 1769, and with their arrival and ostensible necessity for more and more farming land, conflicts began to arise over land.

The Treaty of Waitangi was signed in 1840, between the British Government and the Maori people, in an attempt to ensure that Maoris were adequately compensated for their land, but the continual demand for it by white settlers and the mounting pressure among the Maori against selling, led to skirmishes and land wars between Maoris and *pakehas,* particularly during the period 1863–1872. The Maoris were finally subdued by British troops and 3 million acres of Maori land confiscated, leaving only 4 million acres to the Maoris.

Although the treaty was designed to provide an orderly scheme for the purchase of land by the *pakeha* from the Maori, the subsequent land transfers went very little way to fulfilling its intent. Acreage bought was at prices well below the true value, or further land was confiscated by the authorities. Beyond this cause for retribution as displaced property owners, the Maori people had specific spiritual concerns through their attachment to their lands through their gods. The struggle to reclaim their land now continues as one of the most deeply felt injustices.

Since that time, the *pakehas* have consolidated their position of power in New Zealand, and there are now over 3 million. The Maori population, reduced to 42,000 by disease and war at the end of the 19th century, has grown again to 240,000. The growth rate is 3.7% — twice that of the *pakeha.* Even more significant has been the rapid move from the rural areas to the cities, especially over the last 20 years. In 1945, 25% of Maoris lived in urban areas; by 1971 this figure had increased to 70%. Coupled with this, 95% of Maoris live in the North Island, ensuring major concentrations of new urban dwelling Maoris, a large proportion aged under 21, a result of the rapid birth rate.

Village primary schools for the Maori were established very
early under the Native Schools Act of 1867. Until 1940, however,
Maori secondary education was very limited and tertiary
education almost unknown. Even as late as 1968, less than 3% of
Maoris were awarded university entrance or higher qualifications
compared to 20% *pakeha*. Several studies have demonstrated that
the Maori and the *pakeha* have similar intelligence, and the
discrepancy is not attributable to ability. Two major factors have
contributed: firstly the educational system has been based on a
middle-class European ideology with English as the operating
language, making Maoris apprehensive about total immersion in
such a system, which did not allow expression for their culture,
language or background. The second was the lack of sufficient
financial support, both scholarship aid and funds for research
and teaching of appropriate curricula. The Maori Educational
Foundation was established in 1961 to help Maoris take greater
advantage of the available educational opportunities.

As a result of their educational disadvantage and because 60%
are under 21, they are the last hired and first fired. Coupled with
their rural/agricultural background Maoris are not equipped
adequately for skilled city jobs. In 1966 some 62% of Polynesian
males (Maoris and the 45,000 Pacific Islanders) in the labour
force were engaged as unskilled labour in the manufacturing
industries, compared with 28% for the entire New Zealand
labour force. Banks and other financial institutions employed
only a total of 6 Polynesians; insurance companies 3; and real
estate agencies just one Polynesian.

As in most 'advanced' societies, housing tends to be income
dependent, and low pay or unemployment among the Maoris is
reflected in their housing. In 1966 nearly half the urban
dwellings of Maoris were 'borrowed' or provided with the job, or
rented, (which usually means State rental housing or in run-down
suburbs), compared to 20% for non-Maoris. The Maori and
Island Affairs Department has built homes at a steady rate, up to
1,000 annually in the early 1960's, but this declined to 550
annually by 1970.

Ever since the Constitutional Act of 1852 the Maoris have had
the vote. Four members of Parliament (out of 84) are elected by
those on the Maori rolls. Now, however, with 9% of the
population, the proportion of Maori seats is only 5%. Maori
members of parliament have been appointed to ministerial posts

and occasionally have reached Cabinet status. The Minister for Maori Affairs, a position of some contention, has more often than not been held by a *paheka*. In 1974 however, the Labour Government reinstated a Maori Minister in this position. But the power in both the political and economic sense has lain overwhelmingly with the *pakeha* colonisers. Although attempts have been made to redress this balance, the only integration in practice has been that of Maoris and other non-whites into *paheka* society.

New Zealand, described at times as 'more British than the British', is often described in glowing terms of racial harmony and integration — with few of the problems facing other multiracial societies. More recently, however, more and more evidence of unrest and gang activity on a racial basis, and the substantial clustering of Polynesians in urban areas has forced many New Zealanders to reconsider their descriptions of their society as non-racist.

In 1971, the Race Relations Act was passed to 'affirm and promote racial equality in New Zealand'. It is now unlawful in New Zealand to deny a person 1) access to any public place, vehicle or facility; 2) provision of goods and services; 3) employment; 4) land, housing or accommodation because of a person's colour, race or ethnic or national origins. This may help to prevent more blatant aspects of discrimination, yet it is in a society such as New Zealand's in which positive steps need to be taken to overcome the outstandingly disadvantaged position of the Maori.

Harold Wilkinson

SELECT BIBLIOGRAPHY

Buck, Peter, *The Coming of the Maori,* Whitcombe and Tombs, 1949
Hunn, J.K., *Report on Department of Maori Affairs,* Government Printer, Wellington, 1960
King, Michael (Ed.) *Te Ao Hurihuri: The World Moves On,* Hicks, Smith & Sons, Wellington, 1975
New Zealand Official Yearbook, Department of Statistics, Wellington, 1974

Sinclair, K., *A History of New Zealand,* Penguin (revised edition), 1969
Vaughan, Graham (Ed.) *Racial Issues in New Zealand,* Akarana Press, Auckland

32   The Meo of Laos

In the remote highland areas of Northern Laos, close to the border with China, some of the worst and least publicised violence of the Indochina Wars was enacted, disrupting and almost destroying the society, culture and livelihood of the Meo people.

Of the 4 million inhabitants of land-locked Laos, the Meo (or Miao) comprise about 400,000. They are close relatives of the Chinese, with a Sinitic language and physical features. The first Meo migrants to Laos came only during the 1840s, from Yenan in Southern China, escaping Chinese military expansion and social domination, which included the enslavement of minority tribes. Today there remain two million Meo in China: with the consolidation of the frontier after 1948, the two groups have become separate, like the Yao, a similar group of whom only a few tens of thousands remain. A patrilinear society with strong clan loyalties and hierarchy, the Meo are village agriculturalists, herding pigs and growing opium as a profitable cash crop, and excellent silver and metal workers. Soil exhaustion on their mountain-side farms causes the Meo village to move several times per generation. Lao, from the lowland majority culture, is the common language of Laos, but Meo dialects are retained at village level.

The relatively stable political structure of the Meo enabled the French colonial administration to control the entire ethnic group by favouring and educating the dominant Lee family. French participation in the notorious Indochina Opium Monopoly in the 1890s to finance the colony, introduced refined methods of opium culture among the Meo, who, although forced to sell at exploitive prices, were afforded protection in return from the lowland Lao Kingdom, which had laid claim for centuries to the mountain areas. The French recruited a number of volunteer battalions, which fought with them for the retention of colonialism even until the fall of Dien Bien Phu in 1954.

It was these dispersed mountain tribesmen, who had sided with colonial masters, that the American Central Intelligence Agency sought out and began to form into the 'Clandestine Army' in 1959. Supplying the commander of the ex-French-Meo troops, Vang Pao, with old World War II weapons, and a great deal of money, the Americans built a force of 30,000 full-time clandestine fighting men, and 40,000 reserves of village militia trained by the CIA and Green Berets. During the 60s, territory thus privately controlled exceeded that of the legitimate Lao government in Vientiane. At district level, the CIA troops elicited pledges of allegiance to Vang Pao, upsetting the hierarchy of clan allegiances, and setting clan against clan, although few joined the pro-communist Pathet Lao. Briefly in 1966 Vang Pao declared 'Meo-land' an independant sovereign state, which indeed, might have re-united the Meo in allegiance under him, but the move was aborted by the American advisers.

Soon afterwards, the communist offensive of 1967 swept the Meo from the northern territory they had won so easily earlier, and soon their home mountains round the Plain of Jars were also under attack. The Meo fought back fiercely, but were overcome, to flee with their families from mountain to mountain. The Plain of Jars was taken by the Pathet Lao, and bombed intensively by the Americans, affording no sanctuary to the refugees, who crowded into American camps in the valleys by the Mekong river. Vang Pao himself was protected, but he lost 25% of his army, and with it the allegiance of many more Meo. Civilian casualties will never be known, but 200,000 Meo reached the refugee camps, by the cease-fire in February 1973. Schools, medical services and American example now replaced what remained of Meo culture, beliefs and traditions.

The uneasy coalition government outlined its political programme in May 1974, with the unity and equality of 'people of all nationalities, tribes, religions and classes' among the first priorities while facing tremendous problems of economic reconstruction. Schemes to return and rehabilitate the refugees from all areas (769,000 gathered in Vientiane) were initiated, but

Vang Pao, now commander of the Second Military Region and nominally integrated into the national armed forces, refused admission to the census teams, and only a few Meo were able to take advantage of resettlement. Although the CIA had ceased to support him (but the USAID offices in Vientiane were still seen as running 'a parallel government ... insensitive to Laotian self-respect'), Vang Pao sided with the Vientiane anti-Pathet Lao element, and in May 1975, in what was otherwise a bloodless takeover by the Pathet Lao, he was defeated with the remaining Special Meo Forces. He fled to Thailand, with 25,000 Meo, and later to Paris.

The Meo are dispossessed, ideologically alien and have suffered an almost total social disruption. Few of the younger generation would return to the mountains, although in urban life they feel compelled to deny their ethnic background, while for the older generation the exhausted land provides no compensation.

J.E./G.A.

SELECT BIBLIOGRAPHY

Everingham, J., *The Meo of Laos,* BHP Journal, 1974
Hunter, G., *South-East Asia — Race, Culture and Nation,* Oxford University Press, 1966
Kunstadter, P., *South-East Asian Tribes, Minorities and Nations,* Princetown University Press, 1967
Lévy, P., *Histoire du Laos,* PUF, Paris, 1974

33 Nigerian Pluralism

Nigeria, a huge country whose present borders were decided by European colonial competition at the turn of the century, is not obviously homogeneous. It was administered in a tripartite system at the end of the Second World War, when the country entered a transition period before full Independence in 1960, for geographically it is divided into three parts by the confluence of two rivers, the Niger and the Benue, which form a vast Y-shape. In each of the three sectors lives a large ethnic group with a population over 10 million — the Hausa in the north, the Yoruba in the West, and the Ibo in the East. However, the former protectorate also contains a great number of smaller groups — over 250 in all — who throughout their history have been influenced to varying degrees by the major peoples. The largest and most sophisticated of these smaller groups saw the period of transition as their opportunity to demand status and privileges denied them in the past. Nigeria's contemporary politics have been, and remain, a long struggle to achieve co-operation, if not harmony among her different peoples.

The land varies from the tropical forest of the coastal regions to the dry savanna of the north, and the local economies vary as a result. A central plateau, rising to heights of 5,000 feet around Jos, separates the main areas of population more effectively than the river system; today it is known as the middle belt. Before this century none of its inhabitants, except the Jukun to the east, had ever evolved a political organization greater than the village.

In the north, by contrast, the Hausa states had flourished for more than a thousand years. One of the four great trans-Saharan caravan routes, the Ghadames trail from Tunisia and the Mediterranean coast, led directly to the Hausa lands. Oriented chiefly to the Arab world, the trading cities of Sokoto, Katsina and Kano had developed a rich and uniform culture. Political unification came later, in the form of a Muslim *Jihad,* or Holy War against non-believers led by Fulani tribesmen arriving from the West.

In the early 19th century, nomadic Fulani conquered nearly all of the northern savanna, establishing a series of tributary states. Settled Fulani, more intensely devout than the nomads, integrated with the Hausa, creating a powerful and unified empire. The *Jihad* continued south on to the plateau, even reaching the Yoruba in the west, and many of the weaker peoples of the middle belt were forced to take refuge in the mountains when their lands were taken for grazing.

The inhabitants of the south, with great civilizations based at Oyo and at Benin, were oriented more towards the coast. Portuguese and Spanish merchants conducted a busy trade in ivory, spices and slaves. Suppression of slavery, in fact, was the ostensible motive for the British capture of the Island of Lagos in 1861, but pursuit of commercial interests soon led to conquest of the hinterland. By 1914 Britain had occupied most of what became Nigeria.

British colonial policy had little unifying effect, however. The protectorate was administered indirectly through existing rulers, so the status quo in regard to ethnic balance was maintained except in and near Lagos, which was governed directly as a colony. If anything, tribal differences may have increased, for an element of direct competition had been introduced. The effect of missionary activity, conducted mainly in the south, further polarized the two main areas between Muslim and Christian. By teaching European knowledge it gave receptive peoples — and the Ibo in particular — an educational advantage over the Northerners. It also taught them English, to become the language of government in modern Nigeria.

The greatest problem facing Nigeria since 1945, therefore, has been to reconcile the different interests of the ethnic groups and to allay their traditional fears of one another. When it became apparent that the independent state must therefore be a federation of some kind, the larger minorities in each region demanded autonomy as self-governing states, and the 'states issue' has been an enduring controversy. In 1965, after 20 years of civilian rule, a military coup sought to impose unitary rule from Lagos. This new regime was overthrown later the same year and power given to an officer more sympathetic to minority feelings — General Gowon, an Anga and a Christian from the mainly Hausa and Muslim north.

In 1967, Gowon decreed the creation of 12 states to replace the three regions of Nigeria. The Ibo-dominated east was divided in three. Convinced their power was being undermined, the Ibos attempted to secede from the federation with the entire eastern region — as Biafra. This secession was quite against the interests and wishes of the main minority groups of the region — the Ibibio, Efik, Anang, Ekoi and Ijaw — who between them number more than 5 million people.

Since the victory of the Federal forces in 1970, great efforts have been made to restore the Ibos to the Nigerian community, and to overcome the vexed problem of the minorities. Economic factors will be central to any solution. Nigeria today is one of the world's ten leading oil producers, but her new wealth conceals the fact that agricultural production has suffered severely from the fall in world commodity prices, especially for cocoa, groundnuts and palm produce.

At present, Federal revenue from oil and other industries is allocated to the individual states by a complicated formula which takes account of local needs but is directly related to population figures. A new census published in 1973 showed a population explosion in the north which was violently disputed by the southern states. The uproar was so sustained that the census results had to be scrapped, and the federal government has now reverted to the 1963 figures. Co-operation among the states is essential if the economy is to be developed quickly.

At present, Nigeria is unable to spend her vast income as her economic infra-structure in the form of roads, ports and railways in inadequate to the task. There is a constant drift of population to the towns, where chronic overcrowding and shortage of opportunity have resulted in increased tribalism. The drought in the Sahel forced the nomadic Fulani to move south in search of grazing and brought them into conflict with the settled agriculturalists. With ethnic interests still clamouring to be heard, it is difficult to predict whether the states' governments have the political capacity to postpone regional aspirations to fulfil federal necessities. Despite General Gowon's overthrow in 1975, the promised reversion to civilian rule in 1976 has not been achieved, but is now promised for 1979.

John Gaisford

BIBLIOGRAPHY

Cohen, R., *Labour and Politics in Nigeria,* Heinemann, London, 1975

Hatch, J., *Nigeria: The Seeds of Disaster,* Henry Regnery, Chicago, 1970

Hodgkin, T., *Nigerian Perspectives — A Historical Anthology,* Oxford Paperbacks, 1974

Okpaku, J. (ed.) *Nigeria: Dilemma of Nationhood,* London, 1972

Olurunsola, V.A., *The Politics of Cultural Sub-Nationalism,* Doubleday, Garden City, New York, 1972

Post, K., and Vickers, M., *Structure and Conflict in Nigeria 1960–66,* Heinemann, London, 1973

Wiseberg, L.S., *The Nigerian Civil War 1967–70, A Case Study in
the Efficacy of International Law as a Regulator of Intrastate Violence,*
Southern California Arms Control and Foreign Policy Seminar,
1972

34   Pakistan's Hindus

Only 3% of the sixty-five million Pakistanis are non-Muslim; of
these, about half are Christian, the remaining being Hindus and
Parsees. Almost all of the 900,000 Hindus are to be found in the
province of Sind (population 14 million). They are concentrated
in the major towns and cities of the province, and in the
south-eastern border district of Thar Parkar.

The history of Sind — which derives its name from the river
Sindhu, or Indus — and its Hindu inhabitants, dates far beyond
the invasion by an invading Arab army in 711 and the subsequent
introduction of Islam. As groups of Arabs, Persians and Turks
settled in Sind, the Muslim population grew. Later Sind became
part of the (Muslim) Afghan and Mughal empires; and the
proportion of Hindus in the population declined further.

The British conquered Sind in 1843, and merged it with the
Bombay Presidency until 1932, when Sind was established as a
separate province, and given a form of representative
government. The Hindus, who then formed a quarter of the
province's population, by and large supported the Indian
National Congress, whereas the Muslims backed the Muslim
League. On the eve of independence and partition in 1947, there
was large-scale inter-religious violence in the Punjab and North
West Frontier Province. This led to an official exchange of
population, with the Hindus and Sikhs from West Punjab and
NWFP migrating to India and the Muslims from East Punjab
moving west to Pakistan. Compared to the Punjab and NWFP,
there was very little overt violence in Sind; but the Hindu
minority, fearing loss of life and property, began to migrate
voluntarily to India. By the end of 1948, most of the Hindus had

left Sind. The small minority, who chose to stay behind, seem resigned to constitutional and other limitations imposed on non-Muslim citizens of Pakistan. 'Pakistan shall be a Federal Republic to be known as the Islamic Republic of Pakistan' declares the Constitution; 'Islam shall be the State religion of Pakistan'. Article 41 states that; 'A person shall not be qualified to be President unless he is a Muslim of not less than forty-five years of age'. On the other hand, the Preamble to the Constitution states that 'adequate provision shall be made for the minorities to freely profess and practise their religions and develop their cultures', and that 'adequate provision shall be made to safeguard the legitimate interests of the minorities and backward and depressed classes'. Barring these minor constitutional limitations, the Hindus have equal civil rights. However, a general atmosphere of distrust of Hindus, who are assumed to be pro-India, and certain policies of the government administration, make them feel insecure. This feeling reached a peak, particularly among the Hindus in the border district of Thar Parkar, during the Indo-Pakistan wars of 1965 and 1971, when the Hindus in this area were generally suspected of being the 'secret agents' of India.

As a highly urbanised community, active in trade and commerce and the civil service, the Hindus of Sind have had a high rate of literacy, which they have maintained since the establishment of Pakistan. Under the government quota for the minority communities in institutions of higher education, a *de facto* discrimination occurs when, despite good academic performances, many Hindu students are unable to secure places in university colleges, merely because they exceed this quota.

As Sindhis of long standing, the Hindus tend to align themselves, politically and culturally, with those elements in Sind politics who favour greater autonomy for the provinces and greater opportunities for linguistic minorities, and thus stand apart from the Muslim immigrants from India who came to Sind during and after 1947. This exposes them to the possibility of becoming scapegoats in any struggle that might develop between the Punjabi-Urdu speaking majority and others. However, as of now, the prospect of the Hindus of Sind suffering deliberately planned violence against them seems remote.

As a community which has made an immense contribution to the literature and folklore of Sind, the Hindus remain valuable to all those who cherish Sindi language and literature. While identifying with Pakistan, they continue to play their traditional role in the trade, commerce and civil service of their province.

D.K.H.

SELECT BIBLIOGRAPHY

Abbott, J., *Sind: A Re-interpretation of the Unhappy Valley,* Oxford University Press, London, 1924
Baloch, N.B.K., *The Sindhi Folklore Project,* Sindhi Adabi Board, Hyderabad, 1960
Lambrick, H.T., *Sind: A General Introduction,* Sindhi Adabi Board, Hyderabad, 1964
Lambrick, H.T., *Sind Before the Muslim Conquest,* Sindhi Adabi Board, Hyderabad, 1973
Storely, H.T., *The Gazetter of West Pakistan, The Former Province of Sind,* Islamabad, 1968

35   The Pashtoons (Pathans) of Pakistan

Popularly known as the Pathans, the nine million Pashto-speaking people of Pakistan (population, 64.9 million in 1972), are concentrated in the North West Frontier Province and the adjoining tribal areas, where they account for three-quarters of the population — and in Baluchistan where they form a quarter of the inhabitants. The Pashtoons (or Pathans) are of Turko-Iranian stock, and are divided into various tribes and clans. In ancient times, the NWFP, which includes the strategic Khyber Pass, was known as Gandhara, and formed part of the Iranian empire until 327 BC. Later it was conquered by the Greeks, Indians, Huns etc., but the arrival of the Turks in 988 AD. marked the beginning of the Islamic era. The Turks were displaced by the Afghans, whose Indian empire succumbed to the attacks by the Mughals. They in turn were overthrown by the British, who established their suzerainty over this region in 1849, and merged it into the already existing (British) Punjab.

It was not until 1901 that the North West Frontier Province was set up as a separate entity, and only in 1936 that the province was given autonomy and some form of popular government. Pashtoon nationalist sentiment against British rule had by then crystallised around the Khudai Khizmatgar movement, (literally Servants of God), led by Abdul Ghaffar Khan, a prominent leader of the Indian National Congress. In the elections, held on a limited franchise of 1937 and 1945, the Congress, led by Abdul Ghaffar Khan, emerged as the most popular party, with the Muslim League, demanding partition and creation of Pakistan, trailing behind.

Soon after the founding of Pakistan in 1947, Abdul Ghaffar Khan went into exile in neighbouring Afghanistan, and demanding the formation of an independent Pakhtoonistan to include the NWFP, the neighbouring tribal belt, and northern Baluchistan. This demand had, and still has, the support of the Afghanistan government.

Within Pakistan, the National Awami Party, established in 1957, led among others by Wali Khan, son of Abdul Ghaffar Khan, agitated for the breakup of the West Pakistan Province which had been formed in 1955. When this was achieved in 1970, the party demanded regional autonomy for the provinces, including (the then) East Pakistan. In the 1970 elections, held on the basis of universal suffrage, the National Awami Party won 19% of the popular vote and a third of the seats in the provincial assembly of the NWFP, and emerged as the largest single party.

The breakaway of East Pakistan and its re-emergence as Bangladesh in December 1971, caused an upsurge in the regional sentiments of the linguistic minorities in (West) Pakistan — the Pathans, Baluchis, and Sindhis — who form nearly a third of the national population. As a measure to stem this tide, the central government discontinued the collection of information on the mother tongue of its nationals when it conducted the decennial census in 1972.

There is evidence of growing resentment among the Pathans against the teaching of Urdu to their children as the first language. At the same time efforts are being made to overcome the limitations of Pashto which lacks a script and literacy tradition. A modified version of the Persian script is being used to commit the rich oral tradition of Pashto to a written form.

In the tribal belt, the Pathan tribes continue to rule themselves according to their traditional customs and institutions, with a *jirgah,* Council of Elders, under *Pashtoonwali* (i.e. the Pathan way of life), which is based on the three major principles of *badal* (i.e. revenge), *nanawatai* (i.e. right to seek asylum), and *maelmastya* (i.e. extending hospitality to strangers). A hardy and intensely religious people, the Pathans take pride in their folklore, which stresses bravery and ethical behaviour.

It seems likely that the nationalist Pathans' efforts to establish Pashto as a formal, written language, and to have it prescribed as the first language to be taught to Pashto-speaking children, (which is at present the case with the Sindhi-speaking students), will succeed in the not-too-distant future. The creation of an independent Pakhtoonistan, however, seems unlikely to be achieved.

D.K.H.

SELECT BIBLIOGRAPHY

Ahmed, A.S., *Millennium and Charisma among Pathans,* International Library of Anthropology, 1975
Ahmed, F., (Ed.): *Focus on Baluchistan and Pushtoon Question,* People's Publishing House, Lahore, 1975
Barth, F., *Political Leadership Among Swat Pathans,* Athlone Press, London, 1959
Dichter, David., *The North-West Frontier of West Pakistan,* Clarendon Press, London, 1967
Dovie, Sir J., *The Punjab, NWFP, and Kashmir,* Cambridge University Press, London, 1932
Hussain, M., *A Socio-Economic Survey of Village Baffa,* University of Peshawar, Peshawar, 1958
Tyler, F.W.K., *Afghanistan,* Oxford University Press, London, 1953

36   The Philippine Moslems

The 7,112 islands that constitute the Philippines, contain a population of about 40 million — growing at a rate of 3.3 per cent per annum — which is largely Malay, mixed with Arab, Spanish, Japanese and American blood, but also includes 500,000 Chinese and 80 other minority tribal groups, with as many languages, besides Tagalog (Filipino), Spanish and American English. Of this, the only Christian state in Asia, whose national sports have been described severally as cock fighting, beauty contests, *jai ilai,* and anarchy, Moslems constitute some 9%. Divided into 66 provinces, and these into *poblaciones* (urban boroughs) and *barrios* (villages), each with its own police force, taxes and political 'boss', the country is, nevertheless, theoretically centralised by its presidential constitution and the influence of a few hundred large land-owning families, whose purses are capable of supporting a tradition of private 'vigilante' groups and vote purchase.

The 3–4 million Moslems are based predominantly in the South, in the second largest island, Mindanao — rich in timber, citrus, rubber and copra — and the Sulu archipelago, which curves across the South China Seas towards Moslem Sabah in Malaysia. There are four main language groups, the Maquindanaos and Maranaos of the mainland, and the Samals and Tausogs among the islands. Arab contact with the Phillipines preceded the advent of the Spanish by a millenium, and Islam spread quickly along established Asian trade routes in the 8th century. Spanish rule commenced in the 16th century, adapting the Islamic social structure of Sultan, *Datu* (headman) and community to its autocratic own, and bringing various religious orders, who eventually succeeded in converting all but the remotest islands and the fiercely independant Sultanate of Sulu. Thence began four hundred years of conflict. Labelled 'Moros' like their Moroccan-Arab co-religionists recently expelled from the Spanish homeland, the Moslems in the South were subject to repeated attempts to bring them fully under Spanish administration, cultural domination and Roman Catholicism, which they resisted with varying success over the years.

During the 19th century, increasing contact with Europe and liberal ideas lead to the Revolution of 1896, and the Spanish-American war of 1898 when the United States 'liberated' the Philippines from the Spanish but stayed to colonise in their place. In 1902 they introduced a Bill of Rights, an Education Bureau in 1903, and a superstructure for a gradually Filipinised civil service, but they made no changes to land tenure, and presented the Filippinos with free enterprise, controlled from Washington. The Sultan of Sulu, freed from Spanish imprisonment by the Americans, prevented the spread of these non-Islamic influences in his archipelago.

The Depression reduced U.S. interest in responsibility towards the Philippines, a Constitution was enacted in 1935 anticipating independance in ten years, with strong protective clauses for American economic and military interests. The Second World War intervened, and the Japanese invaders, initially seeing themselves as 'liberators' were resisted by guerilla groups on Luzon and other northern islands, while they never succeeded in penetrating Mindanao.

The 4th of July 1946 brought independence, and rehabilitation, but no badly needed social or land-tenure reforms; from this lack grew the Hukbalahal rebellion on Luzon, which was resisted by land-owners' vigilantes, the local police and the army with U.S. encouragement. In the 1950s, however, President Magsaysay gradually pacified the Huks, and moved several thousand landless Christian families from over-populated Luzon to Mindanao and Palawan for permanent settlement on uncultivated land; and the southward drift continued throughout the following decade, trebling the population in some areas.

Early in 1970, violence broke out in Cotabato province of Mindanao over the alienation of patrimonial but untitled land to Christian immigrants; disputes arose over the interpretation of tenure granted by the feudal *Datus* but resented by the Moslem community, who re-established squatters settlements on land now being cultivated by Christian farmers. Mutual resentment quickly bred the illegal but traditional protective squads — Moro 'blackshirts' or *'barracudas';* Christian 'rats' — sometimes supported by, sometimes opposed by, the local police. President Marcos, re-elected in 1969, was facing increasing rural rebellion, urban bombings and political dissidence on Luzon island (the largest and most developed, upon which Manila and Quezon City and the U.S. bases are situated) from a variety of opposition groups, left and right. Only after a year with close to 1,000 Christians and Moslems killed in Mindanao, did he call a ceasefire to 'find a solution' but a week later ordered troops to resume fighting.

In June 1971, 61 Moslems, including 28 women and 13 children, were deliberately burned in a mosque by Christians and, from that time, the violence increased annually. Claims and counter-claims of massacres, ambushes, military advances, defeats or indiscipline, and above all, mutual bad faith during the frequent attempts at cease-fire negotiations characterised the conflict, ensuring its continuation. The four Moslem organisations appealed to the U.N., the Holy See, Washington and the League of Islamic States. President Marcos put out peace plans, calling on the nation to 'end all injustices' towards the Moslems which had made them 'feel evicted from their land and that of their fore-fathers by Christians who are more intelligent, more aggressive and more affluent'. Habeas Corpus was suspended in August 1971 and Martial Law established in September 1972. Electoral set-back, increased offensive from political guerilla groups on Luzon, floods that rendered 2 million homeless, and assassination attempt on the life of the Defence Minister, and the intention of introducing a new Constitution perpetuating his own position and abolishing the National Assembly, contributed jointly to this move.

The Moslem position had advanced: from the land issue, through complaints of under-representation in the old National Assembly (3 Congressmen and 1 Senator), bias in education against the Moslems and general economic neglect, to calls for a Lebanese-style Constitution accommodating both religions at all levels, federal autonomy and, even from some quarters, secession. The impact of the despised Christian culture was, ironically, high-lighting the deficiencies of their proud isolation. The issues had widened for President Marcos also: an increasing proportion of his army tied down 500 miles from Manila by only 9000 Moslem terrorists, and thus withdrawn from combat with

closer opposition Israeli policy, if he officially armed the
Christian vigilante groups; the increasing strain of concessions on
the budget, and conflict with Moslem Malaysia over the role
Sabah, personified by the (since replaced) idiosyncratic Sultan
Tun Mustapha, was putatively playing in passing guns from
Libya via the Tausog 'sea-gypsies' and training the 15–20,000
refugees from Sulu. This last problem threatened both SEATO,
irritating Indonesia and the U.S., which in the withdrawal from
mainland S.E. Asia is making a great deal of its defence
commitments in the Philippines.

Marcos met Moslem leaders in 1973, promising selective
amnesty and increased economic support, rebuilding of houses
and mosques, and tourism, and lifting of restrictions on barter
trade with Indonesia and Malaysia. At intervals over the next
three years, with increased offers towards autonomy, amnesty
and assistance always rejected as too little, he treatied first with
the more traditional leaders, later with the rebel commanders of
the several groups, including the Moro National Liberation Front
(MNLF), but disaffection, and defection made negotiations
difficult, particularly in 1975. The former legal adviser to the
MNLF accepted the governorship of Zamboanga City and
neighbouring islands, but was disavowed by Dr. Nur Masawi the
MNLF leader based in Libya. President Marcos did arm a
Christian militia in Mindanao in 1973, and conducted the first of
his annual referenda on the new constitution, explained through
the *Baranguay* (citizen family-groups) assemblies, which he
prefers as political units to an uncontrollable National Assembly.
He also subsequently labelled the rebellion a 'Red Threat',
minimising the religious element to gain U.S. sympathy and
perhaps distract the anti-Communist Islamic states; and
increased army service to one year, advancing, too, the Military
Academy graduation date to provide more officers in a
demoralised and indisciplined army.

The annual Islamic League conferences — always preceded by
increased Moslem guerrilla initiative and Philippine government
diplomatic activity — condemn the government's treatment of
the Moslems but do not call for an independent Moslem nation.
The Islamic Development fund based in the United Arab
Emirates, is reported to have allotted U.S.$ 350 million to the
development of the Moslem areas, contrasting with Marcos's own
U.S.$ 7 million in the same year and compared with the 16% of

the national budget spent on internal defence, and the $ 300 million spent on a prestige conference centre for the recent IMF meeting.

It has been as difficult to access the casualties of the war — variously reported from 100 dead per annum to 1000 per month — as it was to be definitive about the social and constitutional aspirations of the MNLF and other groups; apart from geographic divisions seriously affecting communications, which have prevented the evolution of a single political or military front, the ideological contradictions of traditional Islam — with or without a revived Sultanate of Sulu — with the rumoured alliance with the NPA (New People's Army) in some areas of Mindanao, are legion; while the sympathy and democratic support of the Churches for the many harassed Mindanao tribal minorities as well as the Moslems, are also at variance with the declaimed antipathy of some of the Moslem leadership.

Although external supplies of oil were assured by Indonesia, which frequently attempted to mediate, more mindful of its own secessionists than of religion, Sulu off-shore concessions join the list of essential economic interests, Marcos would not like to lose to an autonomous Moslem state. The timber, citrus, copra and rubber companies, staffed by Christians and owned by Americans, have also protested strongly against Moslem attacks on their premises and principles.

In August 1976 an earthquake and tidal wave killed 8,000 and rendered 35,000 people homeless in Mindanao and the islands, and Marcos hopes that the disaster will bring the stricken together, enabling him to comply with the Seventh Islamic conference's demand that Manila halt all military operations before the implementation of a 'Programme of Reconciliation', which includes rehabilitating the 1 million refugees from the war. It is to be hoped that this is not further indulgence in wishful thinking by the Filipino media which, with Marcos, has accounted for many more 'rebels' being 'reformed' and absorbed into government civilian and military service than ever existed. Other reports maintain that the basic force of 8,000 MNLF rebels is regrouping.

Georgina Ashworth

Select Bibliography

Gowing, P.G., *The Muslim Filipinos: Their History, Society and*

Contemporary Problems, Solmaridad, Manila, 1976
Kolko, G., *The U.S. and the Philippines; The Beginnings of Another Vietnam,* Journal of Contemporary Asia, 3, No. 1, 1973
Osborne, R., *With the Muslim Rebels: First Eye-witness Account to Reach the West from Jolo Interior,* Pacific News, 1971
Phelan, B., *The Philippines: Spectre of Jihad,* Far Eastern Economic Review, May 1973
Pomeroy W., *An American Made Tragedy: Neo-Colonialism and Dictatorship in the Philippines,* New York, 1974

37   The Quinquis: Spain's Last Nomads

The word quinqui, short for quinquillero or quincallero, is an occupational term signifying tinker. (They are also known as *mercheros,* a term they prefer). 150,000 nomads are concentrated in old Castille, the Ebro Valley and northern Estremadura with smaller communities located in Galicia and Portugal.

There is no real evidence on the ethnic origins of the quinquis. There are no physical, cultural or linguistic similarities between the quinquis and Spanish gypsies to support the theory that they are a branch of the Rom, or that they are descendants of the Moriscos who were driven by oppression into nomadism. Another theory is that the quinquis are descended from German coppersmiths who immigrated into Castille in the 15th century attracted by the influx of gold from the New World. The only explanation which the quinquis themselves support, traces their origins back to landless Castilian peasants who turned to nomadism after prolonged famines and plagues in the 16th century had decimated the rural population. Many quinqui words and values, and the sense of honour which still permeate the quinqui's way of life, date back to Spain's Golden Age. These include a feeling of racial superiority, stoicism and loyalty, that have survived in an internally homogenous, exclusive group with a marked preference for close-kin marriages.

Social life is characterised by the absence of ceremony. They do not have marriage rites. Couples are joined together by the simple process of eloping (usually with the family's consent).

Absolute fidelity is demanded of both partners and infidelity is punished by excommunication from the clan. The cornerstone of quinqui life is the family. It is essentially a patriarchal society but with no chieftain. Their vocabulary is a mixture of old Castilian together with words of their own invention and their speech is sprinkled with proverbs. They are usually tall and slender in appearance, have a fair complexion and high cheek bones. The most predominant traits are blonde hair and blue eyes. Quinquis have no formal religion but acknowledge the existence of a supreme being.

The post-war economic crisis, with its concomitant decline in agricultural production, led to massive rural exodus. As farmers abandoned their land and migrated to industrial centres, quinquis lost their traditional customers. The rapid growth of industrialisation (such as plastics) in the 50's, resulted in the decline of traditional trades, while better means of transport and communication all but rendered the itinerant vendor's role obsolete.

Most quinquis have a commercial flare and a facility for numbers, but unable to cope with the urgent problem of survival created by new, hostile surroundings, many quinquis have organised themselves into tightly-knit family units or clans often turning to petty theft, burglary and more recently car theft, for a living.

Isolated and discriminated against, they are the object of biased judgements and stereotyped misconceptions. A possible cause of group stigmatization is the quinqui's defensive attitude towards 'normal' society. He chooses to isolate himself from the community where he lives. Quinqui children are isolated from the rest of the community at an early age. They do not attend schools, despite a compulsory basic education law. Few efforts have been made by educational authorities to integrate quinquis into the school system.

Sensationalist and frankly racist articles and reports in the press have done much harm, and even in prison quinquis are discriminated against. They are automatically classified as dangerous.

Kristina Bonilla

SELECT BIBLIOGRAPHY

Starkie, W., *In Sara's Tents,* London, 1953

38   The Saharauis of Western Sahara

Perhaps 100,000 people belong to ex-Spanish Sahara territory; 266,000 sq.km. in area, it is the most lightly populated country in Africa. By 1975 only one in five Saharauis was still nomadic. However, late in 1976 about two-thirds of the population found itself in Algeria, in refuge from the Moroccan and Mauritanian invasion, begun the previous November. The frontiers with Morocco, Algeria and Mauritania are respectively 445, 30 and 1570 km. long.

The desert's earliest recorded people were the Sanhaja Berbers. In the fifteenth century these were subjugated by the eastern-origin Hassaniya Arabs; inter-marriage followed; Islam and Arabic became the rule. Subsequent expeditions by the sultans to conquer the desert and the western Sudan were either unsuccessful or at best only temporarily in control. The sultans officially claimed these areas but, when pressed to act there by European states, would deny they had the *de facto* power to do so; in fact the *bilad as siba,* the uncontrollable zone, began far to the north, in Morocco's present Nun and Sus regions. The Arab-Berber tribes of the desert did however feel a spiritual allegiance to the sultans, notably as descendants of the Prophet. To this might be added, in times of crisis, a temporarily expedient political alliance, with the Saharauis in the subordinate role. Thus, during the French invasion of around 1900, the desert leader, Ma el Ainin, acknowledged the sultan as his superior for as long as seemed necessary.

In 1956 yet another Moroccan venture southwards was proposed by the nationalist party, the Istiqlal, following the country's own independence. Allal al Fassi's 'Greater Morocco' concept laid claim to the desert south to the Senegal and east into Algeria and Mali. However, since 1884, the nearest zone, the western Sahara, had been in the hands of Spain, as 'Spanish Sahara'. Between 1956 and 1974, Morocco tried political and

132

military tactics to dislodge the colonial power, with the support of Mauritania and Algeria during the last four years. From 1974, however, Morocco's annexionist policy diverged from Algeria's preference for an independent Sahara.

For Morocco's King Hassan the invasion promised not only an increase in territory but also a personal triumph necessary to the stability of his throne, with his restless army well occupied in the desert; he would also take over the world's largest deposit of phosphates. President Mokhtar ould Daddah of Mauritania joined the king, as a junior partner, as much to keep the 'Greater Morocco' threat at a distance as to acquire the southern desert; this would include the best port, the fishing bank, much of the water table and the main iron-ore deposit. President Boumedienne of Algeria has supported the Saharauis from a belief in their right to self-determination, a desire to counter Moroccan feudalism by the spread of socialism, and the need for an Atlantic outlet for the Gara Djebilet iron-ore deposit, near Tindouf.

Within the territory the national and political consciousness of the desert people themselves began to develop with the minor war in 1957–8; the Spanish and French at length defeated a large irregular force drawn from the Saharauis and the surrounding countries. In 1970 the death of a dozen demonstrators at the hands of the Spanish police in the capital stimulated guerrilla activities, with the formation of 'The People's Front for the Liberation of Saguiet el Hamra and Rio de Oro', or POLISARIO, in 1973 Spain countered by the creation of a general tribal assembly and of the 'Saharaui National Unity Party', or PUNS. The U.N. Visiting Mission of 1975 was of the opinion that POLISARIO focussed the majority's spirit of independence whilst the assembly and PUNS represented an ageing moderate element ready for an 'independence' with links with Spain. The administration announced a referendum for 1976.

The year of climax was 1975. Morocco and Mauritania took the issue to the International Court of Justice, both to avoid an unfavourable referendum result and to obtain an opinion which could be claimed to support their already-planned annexation. Under mounting international and guerrilla harassment Spain announced its withdrawal; this had to be trouble free, to satisfy the army's 'honour' and to ensure a continuing share in the phosphates — and yet not appear to treat the Saharauis

irresponsibly. That October the Court rejected both Moroccan
and Mauritanian claims to sovereignty and, in accordance with
the mission's opinion, advised a free choice for the Saharauis. At
once there was a Morocco-Spain 'confrontation', probably
contrived: 350,000 civilians 'invaded' the territory. The dust of
this march hid the main manoeuvre, the real invasion by the
Moroccan army across the interior end of the common border.
The Spanish army having been withdrawn from the interior
immediately before, only POLISARIO was left to oppose the
penetration.

Immediately an agreement was announced between Spain,
Morocco, and Mauritania. There was of course no consultation
with the Saharauis, Algeria or the U.N. Spain at once handed
over control to Morocco and Mauritania; by February 1976 the
occupation was territorially complete. During the four months
fighting the king had received U.S. and French military aid;
POLISARIO had been backed by Algeria and thus had a small
amount of sophisticated Soviet arms. The Maghreb and Africa
were divided over the invasion, with the OAU, Arab League and
U.N. ineffective.

At this point on 1 March 1976, the 'free' Saharauis declared
the formation of the 'Democratic Arab Republic of the Sahara';
the military arm was referred to as the 'Saharaui People's
Liberation Army'. The new state's tenets are socialism, with
nationalisation, and radical social change, notably the abolition of
tribal, racial and caste discriminations and the liberation of
women. The Republic claims to represent both the two-thirds of
the population in Algeria and the third still in the annexed
territory.

Allegations made against the Moroccan and Mauritanian
administrations include general repression of civilian movement,
worse than under the Spanish, with frequent searches, a curfew
from 1700 to 0800 hours, the Saharaui housing districts ringed
with barbed wire; abuse of individual civilians, with brutality,
rape, torture and killings, the placing of Saharauis around
military posts as human shields, the enforcement of homage to
Morocco, its flag and officials; attacks upon refugee camps,
including the use of napalm; and official and unofficial taking
and destruction of property. Independent sources have
witnessed or found evidence supporting these allegations,
amongst them the International Federation for the Rights of Man

and the Geneva Red Cross.

The survival of the republic and its people depends immediately upon Algeria and ultimately upon the interaction of U.S.S.R. and U.S. strategies. In July 1976 the OAU condemned the 'foreign occupation forces' by 29 votes to 2, with 16 abstentions. With Morocco in possession, a negotiated return of the desert is not to be expected. But this could result from a *coup d'etat* against the king or from civil war in Mauritania, since the northern tribes are both related to the Saharauis and hostile to the Nouakchott government. A third possibility is that the territory would have to be decolonised by the king if the pursuance of his 'Greater Morocco' aims leads him to over-reach himself by an unsuccessful conflict with all his neighbours, including Mauritania. Morocco has never yet succeeded in dominating the desert for long.

John Mercer

SELECT BIBLIOGRAPHY

Gretton, J., *Western Sahara,* The Committee for Indigenous Peoples and Anti-Slavery Society, Research Report No. 1, 1976
International Court of Justice, *Western Sahara,* Verbatim Proceedings, 1975
Mercer, J., *Confrontation in the Western Sahara,* The World Today, June 1976
Mercer, J., *The Cycle of Invasion and Unification in the Western Sahara,* African Affairs, October 1976
Mercer, J., *Spanish Sahara,* Allen & Unwin, 1976
United Nations, *Report of the Visiting Mission to Western Sahara,* 1975

39　The Sami: The Lapps of Scandinavia

The Lapps are to be found in Northern Scandinavia, Finland and the Kola peninsula in Russia. No archaeological findings have been able to reveal exactly how long the Lapps have been living in

the area, but it is known that their migrations from the East
preceded the Norwegians, Swedes, Finns and Russians.

It is difficult to make an accurate estimate of the number of
Lapps living today as no census has been taken for the past few
decades, but an old census suggests approximately
35,000–40,000, of which 4,000 are believed to live in Finland,
2,000 in Russia, 10,000 in Sweden and 20,000 in Norway. Their
language — which is split into at least 50 dialects with deep
divergencies — belongs to the Finno-Ugric group of languages,
closely related to the Baltic-Finnish languages.

The colonization of Lappland was initiated by the Norwegians,
but the Swedes, the Finns and the Russians soon followed suit. In
the early days the settlers expanded their territories by
establishing marketplaces as close to the Lappish areas as
possible, gradually moving into the Lappish interior, thus
preventing the neighbouring state from occupying the area. The
taxation of the Lapps through fur-bearing animals, was a
dominant feature of the communication between the Lapps and
their neighbours at this stage.

Before 1500 the Lapps' mode of living was semi-nomadic; they
had a central base, but moved between a number of places
suitable for fishing and hunting. After 1500 the Lapps were
required to pay taxes in reindeers for slaughter. The reindeer
stock which had formed the basis of the Lapps' economy
declined, and the Lapps forced to change their mode of living. A
number of Lapps stayed in the interior to establish a totally
nomadic way of life, while the majority left for the coastal
districts. Today only one fifth of the Lapps keep reindeer, the
remaining four fifths are permanent settlers, mostly employed in
the primary sector.

In 1751 the formal division of Lappish areas took place, into
'common districts', under a codicil attached to a treaty between
Norway-Denmark and Sweden-Finland which is still valid today.
The purpose of the 'Lapp Codicil', called the Lapps' Magna
Carta, was to preserve the Lappish nation in Northern
Scandinavia. It established first, that the rights of the Swedish
Lapps in Norway and the Norwegian Lapps in Sweden were to be
given equal consideration, while, secondly Lapps were permitted
local autonomy, and finally, the Scandinavian countries
committed themselves to prevent the occupation of Lappland by
any foreign interests. In 1826 the 'common district' between

Russia and Norway was formally divided and the border fixed. In 1852 Russia exercised her authority over Finland and closed the border between Norway and Finland to the effect that a movement across the border with the reindeer herding units was prevented. The Lapps' right to exploit the grazing-fields across the borders was removed, rendering worthless the guarantee by the Nordic states less than a hundred years earlier.

Economic resources are plentiful in Lappland: ores, minerals, fish, game, grazing for domesticated reindeer, oil and ice-free harbours — riches which have been, and still are, exploited by Scandinavian and even foreign companies. Despite the abundance of natural resources the area is considered backward, and most of the poverty in Norway, for example, can be found in this area, especially in the area with a high concentration of Lapps — i.e. in 1960 the income per capita in Kautokeino where 90% of the population is Lappish, was only one third of the income per capita for the country as a whole.

The development of industrial enterprises, mining industry, fishing industry, the expansion of hydro-electric power and the expansion of the communication network in Lappland have all had negative effects on the original settlers. Most of the ore resources which have been and still are exploited in Norway and Sweden belong to the original Lappish areas. Where mining extraction has been in areas used for grazing, this has destroyed the economic base of a number of families. 'Lappland's ore' is exported, and refined in Central Europe, not in the area of extraction, which with lack of reinvestment prevents compensatory growth and development.

Lapps who utilize the natural resources in self-sufficiency in, for example, Finnmark — the northernmost country in Norway — find that the expansion of communication networks to these outlying districts have brought invasions of tourists, upsetting the natural balance necessary for survival. Officially, natural resources may only be exploited by the local inhabitants, but exemptions are frequently made. No compensation is offered to the Lapps for damages caused, as 98% of the country is owned by the state. In Sweden, usufructory rights to grazing and water and land ownership have been under dispute in the courts since 1966, and legislation for their protection is proliferating in the face of modern encroachment.

The colonisation of Lappland implied an enforcement of

Scandinavian culture, norms and values as the Lapps were considered primitive and backward. On these grounds the Scandinavians justified the imposition of their own values on the Lapps, and condemned their religion. Educational and cultural policies in Lappland have varied from a strict anti-Lappish policy — whereby all Lappish literature was confiscated and the Lapps were forbidden to speak Lappish in the presence of Scandinavian teachers and priests — to a more liberal attitude, whereby it was even allowed to teach in Lappish.

In 1948 a new line of policy was adopted in the Norwegian part of Lappland. A committee was set up to investigate the problems of Lappish education and information generally, and from its initial recommendations a Lappish alphabet was drafted and published in 1951. Further tasks were assigned to the committee in 1956: to examine the essential problems of the Lapps, and to suggest economic and cultural measures which would enable the Lapps to 'prepare themselves to become complete members of the Norwegian society and to develop themselves within it as well'. Similar attempts to investigate the problems have been made in Sweden, but neither country has been successful so far in implementing policies that ensure equality between Lapps and Scandinavians, due to a lack of determination, particularly in respect of the Lappish language, and predominantly oral literature and culture. Hitherto policies have aimed at integrating the Lapps into a system different from their own. Today, Lapps see the problem as one of fighting against this policy of integration, to prevent the loss of their ethnic-identity altogether.

Laila Kuisler

SELECT BIBLIOGRAPHY

Aarseth, B., *Norsk Skolepolitik overfor den Samiske Minoritat,* Sosialt arbeid Hefte 6 Argeng 43, 1969
Dahl, E.D., *Samene i dag — og i morgen,* Gyldendal Norsk Forlag, Oslo, 1970
Gjessing, H.L., (ed.) *Norge i Sameland,* Gyldendal Norsk Forlag, 1973
Nordisk Nukolonialisme, Det Norske Samlaget, 1969
Otnes, P., *Den Samiske Nasjon,* Pax Vorlag A/S, Oslo, 1970

Ruong, I., *The Lapps in Sweden*, The Swedish Institute for Cultural Relations
Siurianinen, E., *The Population of the Sami Areas of Finnish Lappland*, University of Oslo, 1976
Svonni, L. (ed.) *Samerna — ett folk i fyra lander*, Stiftelsen Kurverksamhetens studieforlag, Uppsala, 1974

40   The South Moluccans: Netherlands and Indonesia

The South Moluccans, or Ambonese, are the people of the islands of Ambon, Ceram, Aruku and other neighbouring islands in the Moluccas (formerly the Spice Islands) which now form part of the Republic of Indonesia. Under Dutch colonial rule the Ambonese (of Melanesian-Australoid origin, much mixed with their colonisers) occupied a more favourable position than the other ehnic groups of the Indonesian archipelago, such as the Javanese (largely Malay), Sundanese, Menangkabau, Achinese and many others. Differing from these population groups who are mainly Moslem, the Ambonese are preponderantly Christian (Protestant) due to the successful proselytizing activities of the Dutch missionaries since the beginning of the 17th Century. Under colonialism the Ambonese were recruited to form the core of the native soldiery within the KNIL, the Dutch colonial army. As a result of these two factors, they identified themselves with the Dutch rulers and assumed a superior attitude towards the other ethnic groups in the colony.

After the outbreak of war in the Pacific in December 1941 and the occupation of the former Netherlands Indies by the Japanese armed forces, the Dutch were interned, together with the Ambonese who were soldiers in the KNIL. During the Japanese occupation the Indonesian nationalist movement led by Dr Sukarno received great impetus as the Japanese needed the help of the nationalists in their war effort, and when Japan surrendered to the allies, Sukarno proclaimed the independence of Indonesia on 17 August 1945. The Dutch, however, returned to retrieve their colony and an armed struggle ensued, with the Ambonese fighting on the side of the Dutch against Indonesian nationalism. In the end, the Dutch were forced to transfer sovereignty to an independent Indonesia, an act that was considered a betrayal by the Ambonese. The latter reacted by setting up a Republic of the South Moluccas (RMS) in April 1950 with the aim of separating themselves from the Republic of Indonesia. This separatist movement was quickly suppressed by Jakarta, and only guerilla elements of the RMS remained active on the island of Ceram.

According to the agreement of 1949 between Indonesia and the Netherlands concerning the transfer of sovereignty, the KNIL would be abolished and the native soldiery demobilised. After the liquidation of the RMS some 4000 Ambonese ex-KNIL soldiers and supporters of the RMS refused to be demobilised on Moluccan soil as they considered it 'territory occupied by the enemy.' Hostility from the Indonesians towards these Ambonese increased so that in the end the Dutch government, to eliminate an obstacle to good relations with the Indonesians, decided to send the former soldiers with their families to the Netherlands. This was meant as a temporary measure, pending further negotiations with Jakarta. The total number of Ambonese who consequently reached the Netherlands was 12,500 including wives and children, of whom 93% were Protestant, 4.5% Catholic and 2.5% Moslem. Now there are 35,000.

The 'Ambonese problem' in the Netherlands has not yet been solved. They are still living there, but consider their stay temporary, and for this reason they reject integration into Dutch society and remain aloof from other Indonesians, although for practical reasons they allow themselves to be assimilated into the national work-force. Most still dream of an independant RMS and are therefore prepared to return to the Moluccas only on condition that they set foot on the soil of a free RMS. They set up a 'Government in Exile' in the Netherlands under 'President' Manusama (a teacher of mathematics in a Dutch secondary school) after the arrest (1963) and the execution (1966) in Indonesia of Dr. Christian Sumokil, former 'President', for continued resistance to Jakarta.

The RMS supporters among the Ambonese in the Netherlands perpetrated an increasing number of attacks on Indonesians, to draw attention to their aspirations — and to the heavy-handedness of the Dutch police, and acts of discrimination, real or imagined, from the Dutch populace. In 1966 the Indonesian Embassy in the Hague was set on fire, and in 1970, on the eve of President Suharto's visit to the Netherlands, the Ambassador's residence was surrounded and occupied by RMS supporters. In December 1974 there were clashes, which damaged the building of the International Court of Justice in the Hague, between the RMS and pro-Indonesian factions; later the Dutch police foiled an attempt to kidnap Queen Juliana, for which 42 people were arrested. In December 1975, the capture of a train full of hostages simultaneous with the occupation of the Indonesian consulate in Amsterdam, caught the attention of the world. Dr. Manusuma condemned these actions perpetrated by the militant Free South Moluccan Youth, most of whom have never seen their homeland but who identify with emancipation movements in Africa and the U.S., and see in the example of Bangladesh proof that an independent RMS could be carved from the territory of Indonesia. The events in Timor (q.v.) also contributed to their actions.

The Dutch government agreed to talks, but is mindful of Indonesia as a market ten times the size of the Netherlands, while the Indonesian government dismissed RMS demands for the release of prisoners and ridiculed the idea of discussion between Dr. Suharto and Dr. Manusuma. In October 1976 there was a battle between 200 RMS supporters and 470 police in Vaasen, in eastern Holland, when the former refused to evacuate barracks, in which many have continued to live over the past 25 years, for rehousing. The Dutch government regards the RMS cause as lost, and perhaps hopes that dispersal will help to integrate the Ambonese, and solve their own embarrassment.

Perhaps the most tragic aspect of the RMS movement in the Netherlands is that there is no substantial support for an independent RMS in the Moluccas at present. This is understandable as the Ambonese in Indonesia have now lived for twenty-five years as part of the Indonesian republic and RMS guerilla remnants have been virtually liquidated. The governor and most officials are Javanese, and although there is not much mutual respect between them and the Ambonese, the Moluccas are not noticeably rich in material resources, so that there is neither much impetus to the creation of an independent state of these scattered islands, nor much likelihood of it being viable.

SELECT BIBLIOGRAPHY

Department of Information Service of the Republic of South Moluccas, *Confrontation,* The Hague

Feith, H., *The Decline of Constituional Democracy in Indonesia,* Cornell University Press, Ithaca, 1962

Grant, B., *Indonesia,* Penguin, Harmondsworth, 1967

Kahin, G., *Nationalism and Revolution in Indonesia,* Cornell University Press, Ithaca, 1952

Kahane, *The Problem of Political Legitimacy in an Antagonistic Society: the Indonesian Case,* Sage, London, 1974

Oey Hong Lee (ed.) *Indonesia after the 1971 Elections,* Oxford University Press, 1974

Paiury, I.M., *The Forgotten World,* Gemini, East Weymouth, Mass., 1974

Palmer, L., *Indonesia and the Dutch, A Study of Dutch-Indonesian Relations 1900–1962,* Oxford University Press, 1962

Schiller, A.A., *The Formation of Federal Indonesia,* The Hague, 1955

41   The Tibetans

Little can be stated with certainty about modern Tibet. According to the Chinese, there are about 1.2 million Tibetans; the Dalai Lama's camp, however, claims a total of 6 million. The wide discrepancy is a result of the Chinese not including the province of Tsinhai as part of the Autonomous Region of Tibet. About 90,000 Tibetans live in exile, in India, Nepal, Sikkim and Bhutan. Most of these fled in the wake of the Dalai Lama, following the Lhasa revolt in 1959.

Tibet has always been considered a province of China, but its extreme remoteness and several centuries of internal confusion inside China has made the country effectively self-governing by the first half of this century. It was ruled by an aristocracy of monks at whose head was the Dalai Lama, believed by Tibetans to be the reincarnation of the Buddha Chenresi. The feudal economy was almost totally agricultural, but because Tibetans live at an average height of between 10,000 and 14,000 feet their staple diet was mainly limited to barley, butter and yak meat. One man in four was a monk; monasteries provided the only system of education and owned much of the land as well as the people who worked on it. Many of the monks carried on private business; some even bore arms, and feuds between rival monasteries were a fairly regular occurrence.

In 1949, following the successful revolution in China, the new communist government proclaimed their intention of re-integrating Tibet. In October 1950 the first communist armies entered Tibet and the following year the Dalai Lama's government was forced to sign a 17-point agreement under which, in return for a high degree of autonomy, the Tibetans promised to undertake specific social reforms and acknowledged that Tibet was part of China. By about 1955, there being no evidence of any serious reforms, the communists decided to take matters into their own hands by imposing taxes and initiating land reform in the eastern part of Tibet, known as Kham. This provoked a revolt, organised by rich merchants and monks, which commanded a fair degree of popular support. Arms were supplied by Taiwan and later (1957–61) by the CIA. Fighting continued into the early 1960s, having spread to Lhasa in 1959. But by all accounts the revolt was crushed ruthlessly. On 17 March that year the Dalai Lama fled to India and over the next few years other Tibetans followed him into exile.

Western estimates suggest that there are now about 300,000 Han Chinese troops and technicians in Tibet, many of them defending the long and remote frontier with India and Nepal. Han Chinese are said to form between 30 and 50% of the population of Lhasa.

Tibetans in Tibet: At least until the Cultural Revolution it was possible to practise religion more or less unhindered. However, all able-bodied monks and nuns were told to leave the monasteries and find useful work to support themselves in the community. Large labour camps were set up to accommodate the thousands of prisoners taken after the revolt was put down. Treatment was very strict but on the whole, fair; most of the prisoners were released within a year. Political meetings were held almost nightly, and at least one member of every family was obliged to attend.

During the Cultural Revolution (1966–68) Red Guards came from elsewhere in China, urging those Han Chinese on the spot to speed up the pace of reform. When they refused, fighting broke out among the two factions of Chinese. Initially the Red Guard faction got the upper hand and went from house to house, village to village ordering the destruction of all old monasteries and religious relics. Without doubt this experience alienated many Tibetans who until then had been prepared to go along with the reforms. Demands appear to have been relaxed since then and freedom of religion was among Four Freedoms announced in 1973. There are also signs that some effort has been devoted to restoring the main historic and religious monuments. A few hundred elderly monks are reported to be living in two of the major monasteries, but no new monks have been recruited.

Communisation of the land began in 1967 and was 95% complete by 1975, according to the Chinese. Yet there have been persistent reports of food-shortages, which are something of a mystery since food production has greatly increased since 1959.

The most conspicuous sign that integration remains problematic is almost complete absence of ethnic Tibetans from the higher levels of the regional government. According to Lhasa Radio, monitored in Delhi, in 1974, of the 56 office bearers on the Committee for the Tibet Autonomous Region — established in August 1971 — only three have Tibetan names.

Tibetans outside Tibet: The 90,000 exiles include a disproportionately large number of men aged 35–45 who were strong enough to make the long journey out of Tibet. At least 10,000 of these appear to have been recruited into the Indo-Tibetan border police set up by the Indians; others are to be found in settlements in Katmandu, Bhutan, Sikkim and India (Himachel Pradesh, Mysore, Mussoorie, Darjeeling-Kalimpong). By and large the exiles, because of their business acumen, have prospered in the countries where they sought refuge. Many of the young Tibetans were educated in Europe or in good Indian schools at the expense of sponsors abroad.

The Dalai Lama has made some effort to set up carpet weaving and agricultural co-operatives; others have set up their own small businesses — mainly restaurants and souvenir shops. The two worst placed groups are the several thousand Tibetans recruited by the Indians as labourers for the Kulu to Manali road, who live in very poor conditions, and the 2,000 Khampas (east Tibetans) who formed the CIA-organised secret army in Mustang, West Nepal. The Khampas were evicted from Mustang by the Nepalese army in the summer of 1974 and now live in camps around Pokhara.

The Dalai Lama's exile government has tried to preserve the cultural and religious heritage with which they emerged from Tibet. Exposure to the outside world, however, has tempted many monks to leave their monasteries; and recruitment has dwindled dramatically since there are now alternative sources of education available for young boys. There even seems to be some doubt as to whether this dispersed community will look for a new Dalai Lama after the death of the present one (the 14th) now aged 40. In the long term it is difficult to believe the older exiles are not the last generation of traditional Tibetans.

It seems unlikely that the Chinese would demand forcible repatriation should India and China become friends again. They have not done so with the Tibetans in Nepal, in spite of their good relations with the Nepalese government. The official Chinese position is that all Tibetans are free to return to their homeland at any time. Only a handful have done so, but it is not impossible that the Dalai Lama himself may one day decide to return. Should he do so, many other exiles will undoubtedly follow.

Chris Mullin

SELECT BIBLIOGRAPHY

Dalai Lama, *My Land and My People*
Gelder, Stuart and Roma, *The Timely Rain,* London
Harrer, H., *Seven Years in Tibet,* Pan, London, 1956
International Commission of Jurists, *Tibet and the Chinese People's Republic*
Mullin, C. *Tibet Today,* Guardian, 6 June 1975. Mullin, C., *How the CIA went to War in Tibet,* Guardian, January 1976
Norbu, D., *Red Star Over Tibet,* Collins, London, 1974
Ratne, D.S., *Tibet (Inside Story),* Afro-Asian Writers' Bureau, 1967

42   The Tribals of Bangladesh

Of the 71.32 million people in Bangladesh it is estimated that about one million are tribal. Exact figures are not available because the 1974 census did not take a separate count of the tribal groups, which are to be found in three widely dispersed areas.

The district of Chittagong Hill Tracts (population 508,000), bordering the Mizoram-Tripura area of India, is overwhelmingly tribal. Here, and in the adjoining district of Chittagong, the dominant tribes are Chakmas, Maghs, Lushais and Murangs. The other main tribal belt in Bangladesh lies in the northern part of Sylhet-Mymensingh area, bordering India's Meghalaya, and the forest area of Tangail district. The dominant tribes here are Khasis, Garos, and Manipuris. The third group of tribes — consisting of Santals, Oraons, Hos, Mundas and Rajbansis — are scattered in Rangpur, Dinajpur, Bogra, and Rajshahi along the border of West Bengal. These tribes — of Australoid and Dravidian origin — are nearer to Hinduism and Hindu society than to any other religious community. This is not the case with the first two groups of Mongoloid stock and Sino-Tibetan origin. They are either animist, Buddhist or Christian. The Garos and Khasis are mostly Christian, having adopted this religion over the past century, while the Chakmas and Maghs are Buddhists of long standing.

The Chakmas are the largest of the various tribes in Bangladesh. More than 300,000 strong, they account for three-quarters of the tribal population of Chittagong Hill Tracts. Unlike any other tribe in Bangladesh today, the Chakmas have sacred texts written in their own language and in Pali, the language of Buddhist scriptures. Evidence suggests that at one time during their long history, their ancestors lived in the Arakan area of contemporary Burma: the Chakma alphabet is related to Shan and earlier Burmese alphabets; and the Chakmas show many affinities to the Shan and Chin tribes of Burma.

During British rule, these peoples were treated in the same way as those in other border areas. They were left to govern themselves in accordance with their own traditions; and their areas were not fully incorporated into the province to which they formally belonged. Furthermore, non-tribals were forbidden to settle in their areas.

The Pakistan government later allowed Bengali Muslims to settle in the tribal zone, a decision much resented by the tribals. This and the gradual migration of tribals into India, led to a gradual increase in the proportion of the non-tribals in the area (a mere 5% in 1947). However, soon after civilian government was replaced by military rule in 1958, the district was declared 'tribal' and non-tribals were again barred from settling there.

When the military authorities held a general election in 1970, the tribals of Chittagong Hill Tracts rejected the Awami League, led by Sheikh Mujibur Rahman. Instead they elected two tribal independents to the Provincial Assembly of East Pakistan and one to the national Parliament of Pakistan. The Bangladesh Movement failed to win much sympathy; prominent Chakma leaders argued that the principle of self-determination ought to be applied equally to the tribal peoples.

The country's present leaders state that 'secularism' is a fundamental principle of the People's Republic of Bangladesh. 'The State shall not discriminate against any citizen on grounds only of religion, race, caste, sex or place of birth' says Article 28 of the Constitution, adopted in 1972. Article 41 states that 'Subject to law, public order and morality: (a) every citizen has the right to profess, practise or propagate any religion; (b) every religious community or denomination has the right to establish, maintain and manage its religious institutions'.

The position of tribal peoples elsewhere in the country is different from that of the Chakmas. The tribals in those districts adjoining West Bengal are in close contact with the mainstream of Bengali society, and those in the Sylhet-Mymensingh area feel less alienated than the Chakmas.

D.H.

SELECT BIBLIOGRAPHY

Elwin, V., *Myths of Middle India,* Oxford University Press, London, 1949

Marton, S. (ed.) *Pakistan: Society and Culture,* Princeton University
Press, New Haven, 1957 (see Chittagong Hill Tribes by Bernot
Lucien)
Mukher-Jee, C.L., *The Santals,* Calcutta, 1962
Playfair, A., *The Garos,* London, 1909
Rafy, M., *Folk Lore of the Khasis,* London, 1920
Sattar, A., *The Chakmas,* Muktadhara, Dacca, 1974
Sattar, A., *Tribal Culture in Bangladesh,* Muktadhara, Dacca, 1975

43   The Ukrainians in The U.S.S.R.

The population of the Ukraine in 1974 was 48,521,000, and the
U.S.S.R.'s as a whole 250,869,000. Not all those living in the
Ukraine are Ukrainians, while many Ukrainians live in other
parts of Russia and elsewhere. Nevertheless, Ukrainians are
easily the largest Slav, non-Russian national group within the
U.S.S.R.

'Ukraine' means 'borderland', a reminder that the country has
no natural frontiers and has fallen subject to a succession of
invaders. Kiev, the Ukrainian capital, remained the chief
custodian of Orthodox Christianity for centuries after
Constantinople fell, and became dependent upon Moscow only in
1654. The consequent policy of Russification resulted by the
mid-nineteenth century in a nationalist reaction seen as a
challenge to the Tsar. So 1876 saw a declaration that the only
material publishable in Ukrainian was folklore: even the Bible
had to appear in Russian. In the aftermath of the October
Revolution a government was set up in Kiev which managed to
remain independent of the Soviet Union for more than a year:
before acceding to the Union it insisted on the inclusion in the
U.S.S.R. constitution of a clause guaranteeing the Ukraine's right
to secede at any time (Article 17 of the present constitution).
Lenin's policy of 'Ukrainisation' gave way under Stalin to further
Russification, and worse: 10% of the population (or 3 to 5 million
people) are estimated to have died in the famine of 1932–3, and
nearly one million people were purged during that decade in

attempts to extirpate any potential nationalist leadership. A further two million Ukrainians and two million Ukrainian Jews died at Nazi hands. Post-war reconstruction, which included territorial additions, faced continuing partisan resistance until the late 1950's. A slight thaw in Moscow under Krushchev did not survive his departure, and Ukrainian nationalists were driven underground. At least 100 people were arrested in 1972 for nationalist activities, though the level of repression has since slackened.

Today the vast majority of Ukrainians either appear indifferent to the present U.S.S.R. government or give it their tacit support. Political discrimination is an issue only for that tiny minority which argues for greater Russian fidelity to the spirit of the constitution, or for more autonomy for the Ukraine, or, exceptionally, for complete sovereignty. Similarly, there is no conclusive evidence of any serious economic discrimination against Ukrainians, although the Ukraine does contribute more to the U.S.S.R. exchequer than it receives from it, and it does suffer from localised rural unemployment and consequent migration of labour and demographic imbalance.

In education there is certainly institutionalised discrimination. Russian is the language of science, technology and progress, and so there are strong administrative, economic and social pressures on pupils to learn it rather than Ukrainian. And even in Ukrainian-language schools, the history and culture taught are Russian. Outside school all Komsomol activities are conducted in Russian, and professional, secondary technical and higher education have been almost completely Russified. Discriminatory admission procedures can make it harder for Ukrainians to enter higher education, and the percentage of admissions to applications in the Ukraine is higher for Russians than for Ukrainians. The mass media are heavily biased in favour of Russian, and a further impetus towards destruction of national identity is given by the use of Russian in the army (obligatory for all fit males). The available evidence strongly suggests that education is being used again deliberately as an instrument of Russification. Ukrainian is the official language of the Republic only on paper, unlike the languages of Georgia, Armenia and Azerbaijan. There is a gradual but persistent decline in the number of those who consider Ukrainian their native tongue, and increasingly it is regarded as the language of the lower strata of society. The production of Ukrainian-language printed matter shows a similar decline.

Culturally, a pattern of discrimination — crude and subtle by turns — has been discernible since the 1930's. Official attitudes to Ukrainian culture vary from the patronising through the indifferent and the negligent to the outright discriminatory, with censorship still a reality, even in the case of the great Ukrainian poet Shevchenko (1814–1869), whose work was also censored by the Tsars. A high proportion of those who have been in conflict with the authorities recently have been cultural workers, especially writers. An illustration is the case of Dr. V.N. Skripka, removed from the Kiev Institute of Art History, Folklore and Ethnography in 1971 and obliged to work as a bibliographer because of his article 'Stylistic Traits of Ukrainian Songs'. The many convicted of anti-Soviet agitation and propaganda have received sentences which demonstrate official determination to discourage any sign of nationalist awareness.

Religious discrimination has slackened since Krushchev's time. The Ukraine is the Bible-belt of the U.S.S.R., with about half of all the Soviet Union's Orthodox and Baptist churches. It is also the home of the now illegal Uniate (Eastern Rite Catholic) Church, of Seventh Day Adventists and of many Jews. In 1955 Kiev had 26 Orthodox churches; by 1960 it had eight. As recently as 1973 churches were closed in Chernigov and Zhitomir. Few current individual cases of religious discrimination are known, except that of Father Vasily Romanyuk, now serving a second ten-year prison sentence in a special regime camp, where he is forbidden to have a Bible. The Uniate Church has ceased to have a separate existence, its churches and adherents passing into Orthodox hands in many cases after a state campaign for the 'reunification' of the two churches. Uniate allegiance to Rome has made it a hunted church, with severe penalties for believers. The Baptists, with their allies the Evangelicals, Pentecostals and Mennonites, have achieved a relatively privileged status, except for a breakaway group, one of whose leaders, Georgiy Vins, has become well known in the West. He is now serving five years in a strict regime labour camp in Eastern Siberia, where his health is poor. Ukrainian Jews, too, have had to bear their share of Soviet anti-Semitism.

It seems likely that the twin forces of nationalism and the human rights movement will continue to press, under the leadership of a small number of people, for greater autonomy for the Ukraine, and that they will continue to be met by official resistance, fearful of the strategic implications for the U.S.S.R. of Ukrainian secession.

Peter Hodges

SELECT BIBLIOGRAPHY

Allen, W.E.D., *The Ukraine: A History,* Cambridge, 1940
Birch, J., *The Ukrainian Nationalist Movement in the U.S.S.R. Since 1956,* Ukrainian Information Service, London, 1971
Brown, M. (ed.) *Ferment in the Ukraine,* Macmillan, London, 1971
Chronicle of Current Events, available in English: Amnesty International
Dzyuba, I., *Internationalism or Russification?* Weidenfeld and Nicholson, London, 1968 and 1970
Katz, Z., et al, *A Handbook of Major Soviet Nationalities,* Free Press, New York, 1975
Simon, G., *Church, State and Opposition in the U.S.S.R.,* Hurst, London, 1974
Vins, G., *Three Generations of Suffering,* Hodder and Stoughton, London

44 Yugoslavia's Minorities

Of all the countries in Europe, Yugoslavia is the least homogenous: it is a combination of six republics, two autonomous regions, eight major national groups, three religions, and two alphabets. In the words of Milovan Djilas, 'the very nature of the multinational Yugoslav experiment spells problems.' the complex issue of national relationships, and particularly Croat-Serb tension, has continued throughout to weigh heavily on the performances of the state machinery, and is vulnerable to exploitation and even disruption by the Soviet Union, or right-wing emigré groups. History does not offer much encouragement for the future of multinational concepts, and today, on the threshold of the post-Tito era, it is clear that having created this almost improbable federation, the Yugoslav leaders want to prevent its disintegration whether fostered by internal or external factors.

Serbs The largest single Yugoslav national group — although still a minority — are the Serbs. According to 1971 figures, there were 8,140,000 Serbs in Yugoslavia or 39.7% of the population of 20,504,000. Not all the Serbs live in what is known as the 'Socialist Republic of Serbia' which occupies Yugoslavia's heartland. According to official statistics, Serbs represented 72% of Serbia's population of 8,446,000. The minority groups in Serbia consisted of Albanians, Hungarians, Croats, Moslems and Montenegrins. (The Yugoslavs consider 'Moslem' as a nationality rather than a religion.)

To satisfy the demands for some form of self-expression and also to do justice to the complicated ethnic makeup of Serbia, the government carved out two 'autonomous regions' forming part of the Serbian Republic. One of these is Kosovo in the south, inhabited mainly by the Albanian minority, the other is Vojvodina in the north, where, after the Serbs (55%) the biggest single national group are Hungarians (21.7%).

Vojvodina is a mosaic of ten ethnic groups. One reason for such diversity was the desire of the now defunct Austro-Hungarian Empire to settle in the area as many different national groups as possible to create a bulwark against the Turkish push northward. As the area has always enjoyed a form of autonomy and its capital, Novi Sad, was a thriving cultural centre when Belgrade was comparatively backward, the post-war Yugoslav regime decided to continue this tradition by creating an 'autonomous region', but the predominant number of Serbs in the Vojvodina region made it almost mandatory to place it within the Serbian Republic.

The problem of Kosovo, where the Albanians make up 73.8% of the province's population of 1,243,000 and the Serbs only 18.4%, was of a different nature. To most Serbs, Kosovo is part of their heartland. It was there that the Battle of Kosovo Plain was fought against the Turks in 1389. To exclude Kosovo from Serbia, even in such a tightly controlled set-up as the Yugoslav federation, would be anathema to most Serbs.

Serbia lies virtually in the centre of the Balkans. The Serbs setted in the Balkan Peninsula in the 7th century and by the 12th century established their own state which reached the height of its power in the 14th century. From the mid-15th century until early 1800s Serbia was occupied by the Ottoman Turks. After a series of bloody uprisings, Serbia was granted autonomy within the Ottoman Empire in 1815. In 1878 it was recognised as an independent principality, becoming a kingdom four years later. After the Balkan Wars of 1912 and 1913, Serbia expanded its territory. Following the assassination of Austrian Archduke Franz Ferdinand in Sarajevo in June, 1914, Serbia defied an Austrian ultimatum and was attacked by the central powers. The incident triggered World War I and after much bloodshed and torment left Serbia in the role of a victorious country when a new map of Europe was drawn up at Versailles.

Fiercely nationalistic and proud of their heritage, the Serbs were the main inspiration for the creation of the kingdom of the 'Serbs, Croats and Slovenes' after World War I. It is thus understandable that they dominated the kingdom which later became known as Yugoslavia. The predominantly Serbian character of the pre World War II Yugoslavia led to considerable tension, particularly with the Croats to the west. After World War II, a consistent effort was made to limit Serbian influence for the benefit of other Yugoslav minority groups. Still many Serbs resent their diminished influence. They feel they have sacrificed a lot for the sake of the Federation — during and after the war — and are generally not tolerant of the other minority groups' demands for greater independence from Belgrade.

Croats The second largest national block in Yugoslavia is represented by the Croats. In 1971 they numbered 4,520,000 or 22% of the population. However only 80% of all Croats live in the 'Socialist Republic of Croatia', an area of 21,829 square miles with a population of 4,422,000. The biggest minority in Croatia are Serbs with 14.2%. During World War II, when Croatia was a Nazi puppet state, the Serbian minority was persecuted and decimated. The memories of that infamous period linger on, compounded by reprisals against Croats by Serb partisan units. Even today some Croats point to skeletons of Catholic churches where avenging Serbs burned Croats accused of collaborating with the occupying forces.

Like Serbs, the Croats settled in what today is Yugoslavia in the 7th century, but an independent Croat state lasted only until 1102. From then on the area known as Croatia belonged first to

Hungary and then to the Austro-Hungarian Empire. The architecture of Croat cities bears a distinct Viennese imprint.

Croatia's assets are many. They include the incomparable Dalmatian coast, the country's main tourist attraction, a high rate of literacy and education and a modern infrastructure. Croatia is responsible for 50% of Yugoslavia's foreign trade and is the major foreign currency earner, largely because of the massive influx of tourists. This has been a source of constant tension. In brief, the Croats resent the fact that they have to share their revenue with the other republics and the slogan 'keep our earnings home' has a large popular appeal.

The so-called 'Croat problem' is a source of constasnt concern to Yugoslav rulers. Croats are Catholic and the latent Croat nationalism is compounded by the deep suspicion that Orthodox Serbs are always capable of making a deal with the Soviet Union when under pressure. Croat nationalists who dare to manifest themselves continue accusing Serbs of 'empire building' at the expense of the other minority groups, particularly Croatia. While some fringe groups demand outright independence, claiming Croatia could be just as viable as Denmark or Norway, the bulk of the population is inclined toward a greater degree of autonomy. The complicated population makeup of the Republic would make any concept of independence unviable short of massive expulsions of Serbs which Belgrade would not be likely to tolerate.

Croat demands for greater economic and political autonomy led to mass demonstrations in 1971 which set the scene for radical party and administration purges. Tito himself warned at that time that the country was on the brink of civil war. The Croat purges were followed by similar ones in Serbia as the government tried to avoid the stigma of vendetta against any single national group.

Until a high-jacking by emigré Croats in 1976 Croatia offered a picture of superficial contentment and comparative prosperity to the outside world. But under this facade tensions and frustrations continued to simmer. Should an opportunity arise, Croat nationalism is likely to become an explosive force.

As long as many Croats continue to feel that their national aspirations are not being satisfied by the central power in Belgrade, the Croat problem will remain one of the biggest threats to the Yugoslav Federation. In fact, some Serbian leaders feel that when Tito leaves the scene more concessions to keep the Croats happy will be necessary. This view, however, has a number of opponents, who feel that further decentralisation and liberalisation can only speed the splitting of the artificial Yugoslav state.

Slovenes Slovenia is the smallest and most homogeneous among the six Yugoslav Republics, with roughly 8% of the Federation's territory (7,818 square miles) and the same percentage of the population (1,725,000 according to the 1971 census). But it has the highest per capita income of roughly $1,600 which puts it virtually in the category of developed nations. The continuing expansion of its economy has forced Slovenia to rely on a labour force imported from the poorer Yugoslav republics. At present some 20% of all persons employed in Slovenia come from outside the Republic.

An important factor is the monolothic makeup of the resident population. Of the total number of Slovenia's inhabitants, ethnic Slovenes constitute 94%. The others are Croats (2.4%), Serbs (1.2%) and Hungarians and Italians. The Slovene language, although Slavic, differs considerably from Serbo-Croatian. The Catholic Church is deeply entrenched.

The comparatively rigid communist self-management system which is Yugoslavia's trademark is allowed considerable leeway in Slovenia, mainly because of its historic links with Bavaria and Austria and a generally western outlook. The result has been outspoken enough: Slovenia produces one sixth of the Federation's national income and one fifth of its exports. It is the envy of the other Yugoslav regions and under the federal system is forced to share some of its income with the less developed regions.

Although nationalist feeling is very much present in Slovenia, it rarely manifests itself in such dramatic terms as in neighbouring Croatia. The reasons are two-fold: the Slovenes are not numerous enough to contemplate independence and the rest of the Yugoslav Federation is a convenient market for their manufactured goods, most of which would not be competitive in the west. Pragmatism, devotion to hard work and inward orientation are the main Slovene national characteristics. Many Serbs regard Slovenes as 'Yugoslavs by reason and not because of their feelings.'

Yet there has been some speculation about the feasibility of

156   *World Minorities*

linking forces between Croatia and Slovenia should the
Federation start splitting. Apparently some exploratory talks of
this nature have taken place, involving even Communist Party
members of both republics. There are no indications that the idea
— seditious to say the least in the Yugoslav context — is being
actively pursued.

Moslems The term 'Moslem' in Yugoslavia is used to describe a
Slavic group converted to Islam during the centuries of Ottoman
rule and regarded as a separate 'people'. In 1971 there were
roughly 1,700,000 Slavic Moslems in the Federation, concentrated mainly in the Republic of Bosnia-Herzegovina, where they
constitute 40% of the total population of 3,720,000. It should be
stressed here that Albanian and Turkish minorities which are also
predominantly of Moslem faith are not included in this figure.

The sole raison d'etre for the Republic of Bosnia-Herzegovina
was to find some form of modus vivendi for the three ethnic and
religious groups inhabiting a mountainous area between the
Dalmatian coast and the federal capital of Belgrade. In addition
to 'Moslem' the Republic's population consists of Serbs (37.2%),
Croats (20.6%) and 2.3% represented by other minority groups.
In a way, Bosnia-Herzegovina is a typical example of the national
tangle of Yugoslavia. It is interesting to note that Bosnian gentry
was most responsive to Turkish efforts to introduce Islam into the
heart of the Balkans, while the Bosnian peasants generally
remained Orthodox in the eastern portion and Catholic in the
west, nearer the Dalmatian coast.

There is no 'Moslem' problem as such in Yugoslavia. They are
allowed complete religious freedom and have no nationalistic
aspirations compared to those of Serbs, Croats or even Slovenes.
The Yugoslav Federation, with subsidies from the wealthier
republics, points out the advantages of the present system to
them.

Albanians Because of its high birthrate — which at 35.3 per
thousand is the highest in Europe — the Albanian minority in
Yugoslavia is growing rapidly. While in 1961 it consisted of
915,000 persons, their number had grown to 1,310,000 by 1971.
Although there are no recent statistics, the government in
Belgrade seems alarmed at the constant growth of a minority that
has nothing to do with the concept of a South-Slavic federation.
In fact, a number of Yugoslav-Albanians are casting exploratory
glances toward the nearby state of Albania — and this despite

some obvious economic advantages of remaining as a minority within the Yugoslav Federation.

Some observers of the Yugoslav scene describe the problem of Albanians, settled mainly in the autonomous region of Kosovo within the Serbian Republic, as the most dangerous issue facing Yugoslavia. It is easy to see why: the demographic pressure of Kosovo Albanians may eventually lead to demands for greater autonomy, thus creating complications for the Serbian minority within the 'autonomous region'.

According to the last available figures (1971) Albanians make up 74% of Kosovo's population of 1,243,000. Serbs represent 18.4%, Montenegrins 2.5%, Moslems 2.1%, Turks about 1% and Romanians about 1.2%.

Despite a consistent government effort to implant industry in the area, Kosovo has the smallest per capita income of any Yugoslav region: about $600. It also has the highest illiteracy rate — 50%. All told, Kosovo and its rapidly growing Albanian majority is a social, economic and political problem for Yugoslavia.

As part of its general policy towards minorities, the government condones and even encourages the self-expression of Kosovo's Albanians. A thriving university has been set up at Pristina, Kosovo's capital, there are newspapers and periodicals in the Albanian language. Yet Kosovo Albanians complain that not enough is being done to foster their area's development. There is a latent tension between Albanians and Serbs in Kosovo, the latter feeling — not without some justification — that the promotion of Albanian self-expression is getting out of hand. The Albanians, on the other hand, feel that their position in the Federation is extremely precarious. Should Belgrade ever fall into the Soviet orbit, the Kosovo Albanians believe their rights would be considerably curtailed.

There are some Yugoslavs who feel that it might be politically and economically expedient for Yugoslavia simply to get rid of Kosovo, allowing its lineup with Albania, which, it should be stressed, has never made a formal territorial claim to Kosovo. Yet, Kosovo is part of the Serbian heartland and a territorial surgery allowing it to split away would have to be accompanied by a dramatic constitutional revision. Even a public contemplation of such a thought would be most destabilising for Yugoslavia.

Not all Albanians in Yugoslavia live in Kosovo. In Macedonia
17% of the population is Albanian, while in Montenegro the
Albanian minority constitutes 7% of that Republic's total
population.

There is very little — if any — intermarriage between
Albanians and other Yugoslav nationalities.

Macedonians Macedonia is a trapezoid area of land in the heart of
the Balkans upon which Serbia, Bulgaria and Greece converge
and over which they often clashed in recent history. Thus what is
known today as Macedonia had belonged to the Bulgarian
Empire, Serbian Kingdom and to Greece.

Today there are, according to Yugoslav figures 1,195,000
Macedonians in Yugoslavia or 5.8% of the population. Across the
border in Greece there are perhaps 200,000 people who could be
described as of Macedonian origin and the number of
Macedonians in Bulgaria is estimated at 170,000. However, it
should be stressed that neither Greece nor Bulgaria recognise the
existence of a separate Macedonian national group. And while
Greece has no claims to Yugoslav Macedonia, on a number of
occasions Bulgaria has made demands tantamount to claiming
Macedonia as part of its territory.

What is known as the 'Socialist Republic of Macedonia', with its
capital in Skopje, covers an area of 9,926 square miles. It has a
population of 1,647,000 of which 'Macedonians' represent
69.5%, Albanians 17.2%, Turks 6.6%, Serbs 2.7% and
Romanians 1.5%. It is a typical example of the highly interwoven
national pattern of the Yugoslav Federation.

As far as Yugoslavia is concerned, the 'Macedonian problem' is
similar to that of Kosovo — potentially it can cause international
complications, mainly because of the Bulgarian claim. Although
Bulgaria faithfully follows the Soviet line and its attitude towards
Macedonia generally reflects the state of Soviet-Yugoslav
relations, there are some indications that the Russians have
allowed Sofia some leeway on the Macedonian problem. Some
observers see it as a safety valve for Bulgarian national ambitions.

Before 1944, the official Bulgarian position was that there is no
Macedonia — merely a part of Bulgaria. After 1945 the
Bulgarian Communist Party accepted the Yugoslav concept of a
'Macedonian nation', until Tito's split from Moscow in 1948,
when they ceased to recognise Macedonia once again. This was,
once more, reversed in 1971 but with much ambiguity.

On the other hand, the Yugoslav government has been laying heavy stress on distinct Macedonian characteristics. In fact a major effort was undertaken to make the local dialect into a 'Macedonian' language, and a government decree officially sanctioned Macedonian alphabet and orthography. There has been a steady increase in enrollment at the University of Cyril and Methodius, and the number of schools at all levels has been dramatically increased.

After the disastrous Skopje earthquake in 1963, Belgrade staged a massive solidarity campaign in favour of the stricken city. Today Skopje offers an impressive vista of high rise buildings and broad boulevards, although crowded shacks and hovels still persist on the city's outskirts. Still, Macedonia is one of the poorer republics and its inhabitants clamour for bigger and better injections of federal capital.

On the whole it seems that under the federal system Macedonian 'Particularism' has been satisfied to a considerable degree. Yet there is some identification with Bulgaria and it is not excluded that it might be exploited as a disruptive element should the federal structure start crumbling.

Montenegrins The mountainous 'Socialist Republic of Montenegro' (known in Serbo-Croatian as Crna Gora) covers an area of 5,332 square miles and has a population (1971) of 530,000. Its inhabitants consist of Montenegrins (67.2%), Moslems (13.3%), Serbs (7.5%), Albanians (6.7%) and Croats (1.7%). The Montenegrins have been traditional allies of the Serbs and their area has been plagued by wars, raids and uprisings throughout most of its history. Even during the Ottoman occupation of the Balkans, parts of Montenegro escaped Turkish control. Traditionally fierce and prone to violence, the Montenegrins made excellent partisan soldiers during World War II and their sharp mountains and deep ravines provided hideouts for Partisan headquarters and depots. The Montenegrins have no quarrel with the Belgrade regime and are not regarded as a problem minority. If anything, Montenegro will probably follow Serbia's lead.

Hungarians The handling of the comparatively large Hungarian minority (480,000) by the Yugoslav government since the end of World War II has been highly creditable. A residue of the Austro-Hungarian Empire, the Hungarians inhabit an area in the northeastern portion of the country, generally in the vicinity of the border with Hungary. Because of its diversified ethnic makeup, the area was made into an 'Autonomous Province of Vojvodina' which, in turn, is part of the Serbian Republic. The population of Vojvodina is close to two million, in which Hungarians account for 21%. Serbs make up 55.6% of Vojvodina's population and the other minorities are Croats (7.1%), Slovaks (3.7%), Romanians (2.7%), Montenegrins (1.8%) and Ruthenians (1.3%). To satisfy various national traditions, the government sanctions five official languages in Vojvodina: Serbo-Croatian, Hungarian, Slovak, Romanian and Ruthenian. Hungarians have a total of 195 elementary schools, a daily newspaper (Magyar Szo) and the radio station at Novi Sad (the province's capital) broadcasts regularly in Hungarian. Some Hungarians have reached positions of responsibility in the Yugoslav state and party apparatus.

The Hungarian minority has few claims to greater autonomy. There are no signs of Hungarian dissatisfaction with the Yugoslav system. Again, the complicated population pattern in Vojvodina would preclude any attempt at linking the area with Hungary.

BIBLIOGRAPHY

Clissold, S., (ed.) *Yugoslavia and the Soviet Union 1939–73,* Royal Institute of International Affairs, Oxford Universal Press, London
Dragnich, A.N., *Serbia, Nicola Pasic and Yugoslavia,* Rutgers University
Mensonides, L.J., Kuhlmann, J.A., *The Future of Inter-Bloc Relations in Europe,* Pall Mall, London, 1975
Singleton, F., *Twentieth Century Yugoslavia,* Macmillan, London, 1976
Tomasevich, J., *War and Revolution in Yugoslavia 1941–45: The Chetniks* Stanford University Press, California, 1975
Zukin, S., *Beyond Marx and Tito: Theory and Practice in Yugoslav Socialism,* Cambridge University Press, London, 1975

Uniform with this volume: Vols II & III price £3.95 each
The Reports already published by the Minority Rights Group are:

1   Religious minorities in the Soviet Union (Revised 1984 edition)
2   The two Irelands: the double minority - a study of inter-group tensions (1984)
3   Japan's minorities: Burakumin, Koreans and Ainu (1983)
4   The Asian minorities of East and Central Africa (up to 1971)
5   Eritrea and Tigra (1983 edition)
6   The Crimean Tatars, Volga Germans and Meskhetians: Soviet treatment of some national minorities (Revised 1980 edition)
7   The position of Blacks in Brazilian and Cuban society (New 1979 edition)
8   Inequalities in Zimbabwe (New 1981 edition)
9   The Basques and Catalans (New 1982 edition) (tambien en castellano) ("The Basques" aussi en francais, auch auf deutsch)
10 The Chinese in Indonesia, the Philippines and Malaysia (1982)
11 The Biharis in Bangladesh (Revised 1982 edition)
12 Israel's Oriental Immigrants and Druzes (Revised 1981 edition)
13 East Indians of Trinidad and Guyana (Revised 1980 edition)
14 The Roma: the Gypsies of Europe (Revised 1980 edition) (aussi en francais) (also in Romani)
15 What future for the Amerindians of South America? (Revised 1984 edition) (aussi en francais)
16 The new position of East Africa's Asians (Revised 1978 edition)
17 India, the Nagas and the north-east (Revised 1981 edition)
18 Minorities of central Vietnam: autochthonous Indochinese people (New 1980 edition) (aussi en francais)
19 The Namibians of South-West Africa (New 1984 edition)
20 Selective genocide in Burundi (aussi en francais)
21 Canada's Indians (Revised 1982 edition)
22 Race and Law in Britain and the United States (New 1983 edition)
23 The Kurds (New 1984 edition)
24 The Palestinians (Revised 1984 edition)
25 The Tamils of Sri Lanka (Revised 1983 edition)
26 The Untouchables of India (1982)
27 Arab Women (Revised 1983 edition) (aussi en francais)
28 Western Europe's Migrant Workers (aussi en francais) (Revised 1978 edition)
29 Jehovah's Witnesses in Central Africa
30 Cyprus (New 1984 edition)
31 The Original Americans: U.S. Indians (New 1980 edition)
32 The Armenians (aussi en francais) (Revised 1981 edition)
33 Nomads of the Sahel (Revised 1979 edition)
34 Indian South Africans
35 Aboriginal Australians (1982)
36 Constitutional Law and Minorities
37 The Hungarians of Rumania (aussi en francais)
38 The Social Psychology of Minorities
39 Mexican-Americans in the U.S. (tambien en castellano)

All reports are priced at £1.20/$3.60 each plus 20% P&P. Subscriptions are £5/$12 for the next 5 reports. A complete set of 62 reports plus a subscription can be obtained for a special price of £50/$110 US.

The Minority Rights Group urgently needs funds to continue and develop its work; being a charity MRG is eligible to receive a covenant if you prefer.

For further details and a list of its latest reports write to the Minority Rights Group, 29 Craven Street, London WC2N.

Index

Central Intelligence Agency (CIA)
115, 116, 143, 145
Ceram 139–140
Chakmas 146
Chin 31, 33–41, 146
China(ese) 32, 33, 37, 40–41, 49, 50,
80–81, 114, 125, 143
Chinese of North America xii, 48–50
Christian(s) 1, 9, 34, 38, 39, 50–52,
66, 69, 75, 81, 84–86, 118, 126, 139,
146
Circassian 51
Communist(-ism) 13, 36, 47, 62, 71,
83, 88, 92, 102–110
Copts 50–52
Cornish (Corwan) 53–55
Corsica(n) 55–57
Crimean Tatars xvii, 161
Croat(s) 151–160

D
Dalai Lama 142
Danakils 4
Danes (Denmark) 60, 154
Devon 53–54
Djibouti 3–6
Dominica 58–60
Dravidian 1, 146
Dutch 89, 139

E
East Pakistan 18–19, 36
East Timor—see Timor
Egypt 50, 51–52
English (England) 32, 43, 51–54
Eskimos—see Inuit
Estonian(s) 60–64, 106, 108
Ethiopia (Eritrea) 4–6, 52, 161
Europe x, xii, xviii, 3, 63, 66, 137
Europeans 12, 25, 42, 48, 57, 58, 93,
112
Ewe 74–79

F
Finland (Finnish) 60, 64, 135–136
Finno-Ugrian 60, 136
Flemish 12
France (French) xii, 3–6, 12, 25,
28–31, 42–45, 51–52, 55–59, 114, 132
Franco, Gen. 47
Fretilin 90–92
Fulani 117

G
Ga-Adangbe 74–79
Gabili 57
Galicians 47, 65–68
Gandhi, Indira 87, 99
Garos 1, 146
Gaulle (-ism) 4, 28, 30
Germany (German) xii, 43, 60, 61,
69, 70, 101–102, 108, 155
Georgia 68–73, 149
Ghana 74–80
Gharb 26
Goa 84–85
Gonds 1
Gowon, Gen. 118–119
Greece (Greeks) 45, 65, 68, 158
Grusi 74–79
Guan 74–79
Guinea-Bissan 44
Gurma 74–79
Guyana 58, 161
Gwilmima 26
Gypsies 130, 161

H
Han 143, 144
Hassan, King 26, 133–135
Hausa 75, 117
Haw 80–83
Hindu(ism) xvii, 2, 1, 9, 17–20,
84–88, 96–98, 120–122, 146
Hitler 103
Hodna 25
Hos 1, 146
human rights—see also Universal
Declaration xviii, 43, 63, 72, 107
Hungarians 152–160
Hutu x, xi

I
Ibadi 24
Iberian 12, 42, 45
Ibos xiii, xv, 75, 117, 118
India(n) x, 1–3, 8, 9–11, 15–19, 32–34,
41, 84–89, 97–100, 120–121, 142–143,
146–147, 161
Indonesia 89–93, 128, 139–142, 161
Inuit 93–96
Iran 15, 20, 68
Ireland (Irish) xv, 53, 66, 161
Issas 3–6
Islam(ic) xvii, 7–9, 18, 24–27, 36, 51,
87, 89, 97, 121, 122, 128

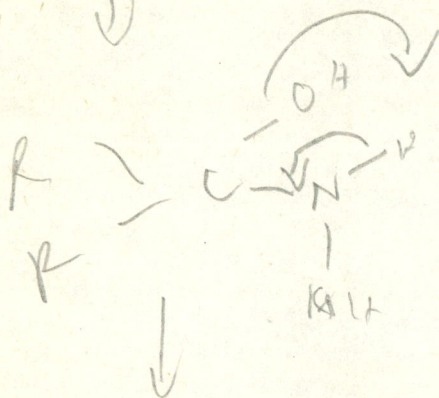

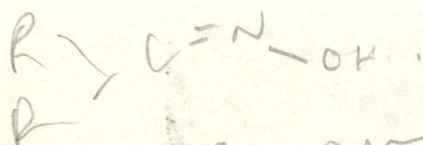

Orange

$R \geq C=0$
H

Yellow

$R \geq C=0$
R

World Minorities

Volume One

edited by
Georgina Ashworth
former Research Director, Minority Rights Group

Quartermaine House Ltd.
Windmill Road, Sunbury, Middx., U.K.
1977

First published by Quartermaine House Ltd. 1977
© Quartermaine House Ltd. and Minority Rights Group
ISBN No: 0 905898 00 1, 1977.

Reprinted 1978
Reprinted 1984

Printed in Great Britain
by Unwin Brothers Limited
The Gresham Press, Old Woking, Surrey

World Minorities

Volume One